MURDER & MAYHEM
ON
OHIO'S RAILS

MURDER & MAYHEM
—ON—
OHIO'S RAILS

JANE ANN TURZILLO

Charleston · London

THE
History
PRESS

Published by The History Press
Charleston, SC 29403
www.historypress.net

First published 2014

Manufactured in the United States

ISBN 978.1.62619.260.7

Library of Congress CIP data applied for.

For Nicholas and Nathan—you are my heart.

CONTENTS

ACKNOWLEDGEMENTS

W riting the acknowledgements is one of my favorite parts of the book. It is here that I get the chance to thank all the folks who helped me put the book together. Without them, there would be no *Murder and Mayhem on Ohio's Rails*.

My first thanks goes to my editor, Greg Dumais, who liked the idea of the book and helped me fine-tune it.

Rich Weller, retired engineer and mechanic for the Indiana & Ohio Railroad and current volunteer engineer and mechanic for the Whitewater Valley Railroad, was always available to answer this greenhorn's railroad questions. His help was essential.

As expected, libraries and historical societies proved to be the greatest resources while researching and writing this book. Librarians, archivists and volunteers found newspaper articles and old records. For an attribution and/ or a modest donation, many of them allowed me to use their photographs. I am indebted to the following for their assistance: Gwendolyn Mayer, archivist, Hudson Public Library and Historical Society, who always gets me started in the right direction; Toni McPherson, administrative assistant, and Beth Marshall, archivist, Logan County Historical Society Logan County Museum; Melinda Ridgway, reference, Logan County Libraries; Bob Cermak and Scott Wade Stone, Cleveland Police Museum and Historical Society; Darrin Upp, president and curator, Society of Historic Sharonville; Gloria Malone, reference/genealogy, Champaign County Library; Nancy Gillahan, Berea Historical Society; Judi Saurers and Bud Davis, Crestline

Historical Society Shunk Museum Archives; Lynn Altstadt, Crestline Public Library; Lynn Duchez Bycko, special collections, Cleveland State University, Michael Schwartz Library; Bob Lyngos, special collections, Alpena County (Michigan) George N. Fletcher Public Library; Christina McVay and Darlene McKenzie, Portage County Historical Society; Holly Hanna, Williams County Public Library Local History Center; Jane Isaacs, public services, Plain City Library; Bernie Vance, Plain City Historical Society; Shalini, Brad, Elizabeth Lang and Albert Hallenberg, information and reference, Public Library of Cincinnati and Hamilton County; Linda Bailey, curator, Cincinnati Museum Center; Richard W. Gross, Greater Cincinnati Police Historical Society Museum; Sue Kienbaum, Marysville Public Library; Angela O'Neal, Russ Pollitt and Nick Taggart, genealogy/history/travel, Columbus Metropolitan Library; and Patrice Y. Hamiter and Nicholas Durda, photograph collection, Cleveland Public Library.

I also want to thank Janet Ketchum Armbrust for information on Joe Ketchum, the murdered baggage master. Kit Sempak, whose grandfather was at the Garrettsville station when Alvin Karpis robbed the train there, sent me information on that holdup. Thank you.

Many thanks to the talented Justin Campbell, who did three wonderful illustrations for me, and photo expert Bonnie Janelle for helping me get the photographs ready.

I am grateful to my sister, Mary Turzillo, and my friend and neighbor, Marilyn Seguin. Both have been my writing mentors and my first readers.

My writing buddy, Wendy Koile, got me to submit the idea of a train-robbery book and then provided support and kept me laughing—thanks, Wendy! I also want to thank the members of my Sisters in Crime group. Each and every one of them has given me inspiration.

This book was also made possible by those period journalists whose bylines never appeared at the tops of the stories they wrote for Ohio newspapers.

And finally, I want to thank my son, John-Paul Paxton, for his love and encouragement.

I hope I haven't forgotten anyone. If I did, it wasn't intentional.

I will miss my Tommy, who laid under my desk while I wrote this book. RIP, boy.

INTRODUCTION

Although most readers are familiar with the train robberies of the Old West and names like Jesse James, Cole Younger, the Reno Brothers, Butch Cassidy and the Sundance Kid and Belle Starr (yes, women got into the act, too), the first peacetime train robbery in the United States happened at North Bend along the Ohio River in Hamilton County, Ohio. The culprits were not famous—in fact, they were never caught, so we do not even know their names.

The year was 1865, only weeks after the close of the Civil War and five years before the first western train robbery at Verdi, Nevada, in 1870. Some historians deny North Bend as the location of the first peacetime train robbery because it was on the heels of the war, and they claim guerrillas were responsible.

Alternatively, they give the distinction of the first train robbery to John and Simeon Reno and Franklin Sparks on an Ohio & Mississippi train near Seymour, Indiana, in 1866. When the total of evidence is studied, the North Bend holdup stands the test.

After the war, the railroads saw a monumental growth in Ohio and contributed mightily to the decline of the canals. Trains were faster and could carry more goods—and they carried money in the form of payrolls and well-to-do passengers.

Just as the clatter of the tracks turned some men into wealthy entrepreneurs, it opened up the occupation of train robber. Some of these outlaws became real professionals. Old western movies and TV programs often portrayed masked bandits—six-shooters in hand—jumping from their horses onto moving trains. In Ohio, at least, it did not happen exactly that way.

Instead, the outlaws blew up tracks or dislodged rails to halt or derail a train. This was how the bandits pulled the North Bend train robbery.

Holdup men all wore masks of some variety and brandished guns. The more professional thieves carried dynamite to blow safes. The less experienced thieves depended on obtaining keys from the messengers. Many robbers threw the safes off the moving trains to waiting highwaymen along the route. They would then get off at the next stop and circle back to collect the spoils.

Most robberies occurred at night. At Reese Siding in Williams County, one road agent waved a red lantern in the dark while his pals hid in the woods. When the train ground to a halt, they overpowered the engineer first and then the express messenger who was in charge of the money. The scoundrels dynamited the safe.

Bold gangsters like Alvin "Creepy" Karpis and his cohorts waited for the train to roll into the station before they made their move in 1935. Karpis, a lover of drama, committed the heist in broad daylight.

Some thieves preferred to climb aboard at the station and wait until the train was moving. This was often the case with tramps. Once the deed was done, they would clutch their swag and jump as the train slowed down at the next stop.

Tramps were a hazard to railroaders. It was common practice for vagrants to hop aboard as the train left the depot and ride in boxcars or on platforms. Although the majority of them were just transients who wanted a ride to the next city to find work, some had more sinister plans in mind once the locomotive was underway.

While there were trainmen who would turn a blind eye to tramps stealing rides, Joe Ketchum, a Big Four baggage master, would not. Known for his bravery, he lost his life in 1888 as he tried to put a gang of four undesirables off his train as it pulled out of Delhi.

Former expressmen- and railroaders-turned-robbers were an especially desperate bunch. They knew the workings of the train and how to get at the money. In 1900, Rosslyn Ferrell killed the express messenger to keep his identity hidden.

Railroading was a perilous business around the whole country, not just in the West. The engineers, brakemen, conductors, firemen and express messengers kept the country rolling in the face of danger.

Out of the numerous robberies and murders that happened on Ohio's rails, ten are recounted here. I hope you enjoy reading them as much as I enjoyed researching and writing about them.

CHAPTER 1
ROB EVERY DAMNED MAN

R ob every damned man, but don't hurt the ladies," growled one of the gun-wielding robbers who boarded the westbound Ohio & Mississippi train after derailing it.

Sometime during the day of May 5, 1865, a gang of thieves floated their skiffs across the Ohio River from the Kentucky side to a spot where the train track ran close to the water between Gravel Pit, the site of old Fort Finney, and North Bend, Ohio. They displaced only one rail, knowing that was enough to stop the train. Then they lay in wait for the calamity to happen.

The train pulled away from the Cincinnati depot bound for St. Louis at eight o'clock that night, right on time. The steam engine, called the Kate Jackson, pulled four passenger coaches with a full load of riders, including a company of Eighth Regulars, a baggage car and an Adams Express car carrying three money safes. About seventeen and a half miles out, it ran into the gang's trap. The Kate Jackson was thrown from the tracks and overturned onto its side, pulling the express and baggage cars over with it. All three were badly damaged. The passenger cars remained upright, but one drove through the end of the baggage car.

The passengers were thrown into chaos. During the turmoil, they heard gunfire arcing over the wreck. Suddenly, the gun-wielding cutthroats filled the doorways of the coaches.

Each of the thieves brandished "fine silver-mounted navy revolvers," according to one of the passengers. No rifles were in evidence, but some of the desperados were armed with as many as four weapons.

An Ohio & Mississippi train, circa 1865. *Cincinnati Museum Center.*

The exact number of robbers was lost during the confusion, but newspaper reports placed the count between fifteen and twenty. All but one wore civilian clothing. That exception was dressed in something resembling a uniform, but no one said whether it was Union or Confederate. One of the desperados answered to lieutenant and one to captain. They were remarkably villainous in bearing and action, according to an article in the *Cincinnati Daily Enquirer.* They barked orders at the passengers to surrender their valuables. One stood guard at each door while others walked through the train collecting watches, diamond stickpins and money.

None of the soldiers in the Eighth Regulars was armed, so they were powerless to defend the train. The ruffians passed by them but stopped by one soldier who was returning home from the war.

"Empty your pockets—now," one of the thieves snarled at the soldier.

The soldier's hands shook as he dug into his pockets and came out with $300. "Let me keep part of my money. Please," he begged. "I'll need it when I get home."

The robber leveled his gun at the young man's forehead. "Hand it over!"

The conductor, Mr. Shepard, tried to resist, so one of the robbers shot at him but missed either purposely or because he was a bad shot. Shepard wound up handing over $40 but saved $320 by dropping it through a hole in his coat pocket. One fellow lost $500 in greenbacks, while another lost $200, his watch and a valuable breast pin. The engineer relinquished a valuable watch.

Paul B. Clark was on his way out west. A lumberman by trade, hailing from Allegheny County, New York, Clark had floated down the river on a raft to Cincinnati. He dislocated his hip during the derailment, but the robbers showed no pity and took what cash he had—about $70.

The thieves were more generous to a young army captain who suffered several broken ribs during the wreck.

"How bad are you hurt?" the robber asked in a softer tone.

"I think it's bad," the captain cried, holding his one side.

"You got any money?"

"Six, maybe seven dollars is all."

The bandit stood looking at him for a minute as if assessing him and then said, "Keep it. You'll likely need it."

Passengers in the sleeping coach had time to hide their valuables before the bandits got around to that car. Ladies dropped their jewelry down the front of their bodices or hid their money in their skirts. One shrewd woman unrolled her elaborate hairdo and rerolled it with her diamond rings and earrings along with $2,000 in cash and her husband's gold watch tucked neatly inside. Just so the thieves would not be suspicious at their lack of valuables, she and her husband left a few dollars out.

Another bumbling gentleman had the wherewithal to hide a watch of little value down his pant leg but didn't think about the $2,000 in his coat pocket. He lost his money but kept the cheap watch.

While the majority of the gang was collecting valuables from the passengers—or their "ticket equivalent," as one of the robbers called it—five others went to the express car. It had tipped over on its side, trapping the messenger, Mr. Pierce. When Pierce poked his head out to see what all the commotion was, one of the robbers greeted him with the threat to "blow the top of your head off if you don't get back inside."

The robbers used an axe to hack their way into the car, where they demanded the keys to the three safes. Pierce explained that he had only one set and that was for the local safe. The other two safes on board were "through" safes from Cincinnati to St. Louis, and he had no way of getting into them. Undaunted by the lack of keys, the thieves first tried to hack the safes open with the axe but fell back on gunpowder to blast them open.

The whole derailment and robbery took about an hour. The ensuing investigation turned up a fisherman who saw the entire thing from a hut near the river. He witnessed the ruffians come across the river on four skiffs from the Kentucky side during the day. After the holdup, the fisherman saw the robbers steal away with their plunder on their skiffs back to the Kentucky side.

Before daylight, a sixty-man military detachment from Lawrenceburg, Indiana, rode out to hunt down the robbers. On the Kentucky shore near Covington, they found a farmer who presumed two of his missing horses were taken by the thieves. The military tracked the robbers farther south to Verona, Kentucky. Authorities were told of a dozen men seen carousing and spending wildly, but no one was giving names.

The next day, Adams Express posted a $500 reward "for each and every person arrested and convicted" in connection with the robbery of the passengers and express and the derailing of the Ohio and Mississippi train.

The company released what it had lost during the robbery. Among other securities and valuables stolen were twenty U.S. 7-30 coupon bonds of $500 each and ten U.S. 7-30 coupon bonds of $1,000 denomination each. These numbered bonds were property of the U.S. Treasury Department, and the public bankers and brokers were especially warned against purchasing them.

Military authorities suspected it was the work of Rebel guerrillas who refused to give up the Confederate cause. The country was still reeling from a war that had torn it apart. Jefferson Davis was still on the run, and Abraham Lincoln had been assassinated. Historians do not always agree on whether the North Bend holdup was the first peacetime train robbery in the United States, in part because it happened a mere month after the close of the Civil War.

Today, researchers contend that if the ruffians were indeed Confederates, they would have pulled out several rails on the track in an effort to destroy the train. As it was, they did just enough to get the train stopped. And even though two of them were referred to by military rank, only one was dressed in a uniform. The rest wore civilian clothing. Their choice of weapons suggested they were criminals rather than guerrillas. If they were Confederate holdouts, they would have had rifles as well as handguns.

Occasionally, the title of first train robbery is given to the botched attempt at Seymour, Indiana, but the Reno brothers pulled that holdup more than a year after the North Bend job.

On May 8, 1865, one paragraph ran in the *Cincinnati Daily Commercial* claiming that two men, named Porter and Ellis, were arrested and held by military authorities on suspicion of being part of the gang that robbed the train. Whether these two were involved has been swallowed in history, and so has the gang that pulled the robbery. That same day, the *Cincinnati Daily Gazette* urged employees on a railroad train to arm themselves. The article claimed that if the employees of the Ohio & Mississippi train had been armed, fifteen men would not have been able to overcome one hundred armed men. The writer did say that no one could have foreseen the train being derailed. The article called on the military to "adopt severe measures, and by a vigorous policy exterminate the outlaws." The writer finished with some rather coldblooded words: "A full course of killing is the only efficient remedy."

CHAPTER 2
A MAN OF NERVE

The thought of becoming a hero was the furthest thing from George H. Price's mind as the Pacific Express pulled out of Lima station, where it had stopped for water a little before two o'clock on Friday morning, May 7, 1875. Barreling along on the Pittsburgh, Fort Wayne and Chicago road, the train was headed east, nonstop for Forest, Ohio.

Price, the thirty-two-year-old Adams Express messenger, was alone and securely locked in the express car. The first thing he did after the train got underway was to fill the stove with coal so he could relax for the 160-mile trip to Pittsburgh. In his care, according to the *Chicago Post and Mail*, were a safe containing money and valuable papers and several packages filled with jewelry, diamonds and other costly wares such as silk. The *Cleveland Leader* put the total value at an amazing $300,000. There was never any confirmation of this amount.

A short distance outside Lima, near Lafayette, Price suddenly heard a gruff voice bark out the command, "Surrender!" Taken by complete surprise, he looked up, and there stood a man with a mask made of black cloth covering his head and half his body. The car was well lit with candles, so Price saw two eyes shining from behind the eyeholes in the mask. He could clearly see that the man was pointing a gun straight at him. "Give me your keys!"

Price told his hometown newspaper, the *Courier-Journal* of Louisville, that the holdup man was between him and his Smith & Wesson. "I dodged down behind him and reached for my pistol. As I did so, the fellow fired at me." As

Historic Lima Pennsylvania Railroad Passenger Depot built by the Pennsylvania Railroad in 1887. *Columbus Metropolitan Library.*

Price swooped down for his gun, he was struck with a bullet to the shoulder. He was a tall man, strong and fully proportioned at 198 pounds, so the shot did not knock him over.

"We stood within one foot of each other. I grabbed my pistol with my left hand and immediately changed it to my other, raising the hammer as I sprang into the rear part of the car," Price said.

"As I turned to face him, I saw the flash of his pistol again." The messenger said he threw up his left arm. The bullet hit just above his wrist, glanced off and struck him in the left cheek near his chin. It was life or death, and Price acted instinctively.

"By this time I had my pistol leveled at him, and knowing that unless I fired he might again shoot and perhaps kill me, I pulled the trigger." The barrel of his gun flashed, and a loud report filled the car. The robber fell, uttering no sound. "I then cocked my pistol again and waited a second or two, but seeing he did not move, went forward and examined his body." He was dead. The whole incident had taken less than a minute.

Price pulled the bell rope and stopped the train. The brakeman came back to the car, and Price let him in. "I told him to look there and see what I had done, designating the corpse as I spoke."

The brakeman called for the conductor. After the conductor entered the car, they began to investigate how the robber had gained entrance. They found he had sawed a panel out of the door at the back of the car. The hole was hidden from view by some corn bags that had been pushed up against the door. The train noises prevented Price from hearing the sound of the sawing. The express car should have been immediately behind the engine, but a refrigerator car was in between, and a baggage car followed the express car.

They later learned that the man had taken a train from Fort Wayne, Indiana, and gotten off at Lima, where he boarded Price's train. He most likely crawled over the baggage car to the rear platform of the express car, where he had access to the back panel.

The conductor pulled the mask off the robber's face and body. In addition to the eyeholes, it had a hole cut for breathing. It was an unusual length, fastened around the neck with a rubber band and secured to his body with string. It was made from a lightweight woven linen or cotton material and looked similar to a Ku Klux Klan garment.

"We did not recognize his face," Price said. "We let the body remain where it had fallen, and the train proceeded on to Forrest, Ohio." Price did not have to ride the rest of the way alone with the body, however. The brakeman stayed in the express car with him.

When the train arrived in Forrest, Price sent dispatches to his route agents in Mansfield and Crestline. He asked for one of those agents to take the rest of his route. Because of his wounds and maybe his mental state, he did not think he was capable of completing his route. At Crestline, an agent was waiting to relieve him.

The would-be robber's body was taken off the train. Some of the trainmen at the station recognized him as Homer C. Binkley even though he had shaved his familiar beard. He had been a conductor who was discharged from the Pittsburgh, Fort Wayne & Chicago Railroad two weeks before the incident. He had worked for the railroad for some time. Before becoming a conductor, he was a brakeman. On his last job, he had been running the accommodation train between Lima and Fort Wayne.

Binkley's actions astonished those who had known him for a long time. He was well liked and was a member of the Conductor's Brotherhood and the Order of Red Men, an organization that traced its routes to the Sons of Liberty and with rituals modeled after those of American Indians. Several stories surfaced as to why he was let go from the railroad. The trainmen at Crestline heard Binkley had associated with some bad people, while others said he had "bad habits." There was speculation

Crestline's Union Station, built in 1864, included the Continental Hotel. Abraham Lincoln is believed to have stayed there. *Crestline Historical Society Shunk Museum Archives.*

that he had gambling debts. A rumor surfaced that he had purchased a diamond saw before the incident. He told a number of people that he needed money badly and must have it no matter what. Whatever his reasons were for purchasing the saw and needing money, he left his home in Fort Wayne on Thursday night, May 6, and he was seen at Lima before the train pulled out.

As a former railroad man, Binkley knew there would be a large amount of money on this train. He also knew the best way to get into the express car. He picked the west-end door and waited to begin using his saw on the end panel until the train was underway and the locomotive noises would cover any sounds his saw might make.

The Pittsburgh papers reported that curiosity seekers flocked to look at the car in Crestline. A large number of those were officers and employees of the railroad and express companies. The papers said there was a large amount of blood on the floor in the center of the car, indicating where the shootout had occurred.

Price went to Mansfield, where the railroad surgeon took the slug out of his shoulder. It was determined that the other injuries were flesh wounds that would heal up within a few days. The bullet that hit him in the chin had glanced off and was probably lodged in the wall of the express car.

After Price was patched up, he and the Adams Express route agent, W.H. Damsel, Esquire, went back to Crestline. The Crawford County authorities refused to hold an inquest into the killing because the incident had occurred in Allen County, so the corpse was sent back to Lima. Price learned during the inquest that he had shot Binkley directly over his right eye. The bullet was extracted from the back of the robber's head and found to be slightly flattened, probably from hitting bone. The shooting was eventually ruled justifiable by reason of self-defense.

Once the inquest was complete, Price went home to recuperate in Louisville and be with his wife, Josephine; his two daughters, seven-year-old Lillie and one-year-old Maude; and his son, four-year-old Henry. Josephine had been kept aware of what was happening through telegrams and no doubt was anxiously awaiting his arrival. Louisville had been Price's home for approximately ten years, and he was well liked there by his neighbors and acquaintances. Everyone who knew him was horrified at the ordeal and hailed him as a hero. He was formerly the editor of the journal *Our Expressman* when it was published in Louisville. After a few days at home, he left for Cincinnati for a meeting with the Adams Express directors.

"When I saw Binkley shooting, I was never the least bit afraid," Price said when asked how he felt about the incident. "And I thought only of saving my sealed safe containing the company's valuable packages of money, the amount of which I am not aware of, though it was considerable." The two men were only about eight to ten feet apart as they shot at each other, he said, although he first described the space between them as one foot. The dead man's gun was smaller than Price's Smith & Wesson, and Price was a better shot.

One grisly fact emerged as the body was retrieved. Binkley had an oak coupling block and a ten-foot-long rope wrapped around his left arm and made into a slip noose. Price figured the rope was intended to tie him up or strangle him, but authorities thought Binkley may have had an accomplice and that the plan was to incapacitate the messenger and then throw the safe off the train at a predetermined spot. "It is hard to say whether Binkley intended to kill, but his actions tended that way," Price said. The train was searched, and no accomplices were ever found, so the would-be robber apparently was acting on his own.

Homer C. Binkley was a thirty-eight-year-old resident of Fort Wayne, Indiana, and he apparently had come from a well-respected family. He had two children: a sixteen-year-old daughter and a five-year-old son. His wife collapsed at the news of his death and became deranged. Neighbors and relatives said that his family was left in dire circumstances. His body was returned to Fort Wayne for burial.

A week after the shooting, the express company held its quarterly meeting. The company officials passed a resolution authorizing a payment of $1,000 in gold to George H. Price.

"I regret the affair happened for his family's sake," Price told the *Courier-Journal* reporter, "but it was either him or me to die, and you know what is said about self-preservation."

CHAPTER 3

WANTED! FOR THE MURDER OF DETECTIVE HULLIGAN

B linky" Morgan could have been anything he wanted. He was intelligent and well educated. Judging by his polished exterior, at five-foot-seven with grey hair and eyes, he might have been a distinguished college professor, a minister or a successful businessman. In reality, he was a pathological liar, a clever and dangerous man who chose burglary, safecracking, robbery and murder as a way of life.

Not much was known about Morgan's background, and he apparently liked it that way. He told so many different stories that no one knew for sure which was true. He never talked about his family, but he was born in Philadelphia in 1834. There was some evidence that he had served a short time in the Union army during the Civil War and had lost sight in one eye after an explosion, which is how he got the name "Blinky." In another story, he told the *Plain Dealer* that the injury occurred when he used too much powder on a safe he was trying to blow open. He sometimes wore glasses to cover the defect. Because little was known about him, stories multiplied and had him traveling in Europe and South America, being an English thief with numerous aliases, tunneling out of the penitentiary in Michigan and breaking out of jail in Kingston, Ontario. Some of the stories are true, and others are up for conjecture. He used the names Conklin, McDonald, Carrothers and probably many more. His death certificate reads Charles H. Morgan and claims he was a bookbinder.

Morgan's life was a lot more open after he and his gang burglarized Benedict & Ruedy's Hatters and Furriers at 247 Superior Street in

Charles "Blinky" Morgan. *Cleveland Police Historical Society Inc.*

Cleveland on January 29, 1887. That burglary would lead to the desperate rescue of Harry "Kid" McMunn on a Cleveland & Pittsburgh train in Ravenna, the murder of Cleveland Detective Captain William Hulligan and the near death of Captain Henry Hoehn. Ultimately, Morgan's life drew to a close at the end of a hangman's noose.

Benedict & Ruedy's sold fur goods and hats. The *Cleveland Leader* described the operation as being housed in a long, narrow building on Superior Street that was used for both sales and manufacturing. Because of its shape, the salesroom was dark and needed electric lamps to illuminate it. The basement served as storage for dressed hides. Located in the business center of Cleveland, it was one hundred paces off Public Square in a vibrant part of the city where many stores were open all night and there was constant pedestrian traffic. There was a hack (taxi) stand in front of the store.

Between six and seven o'clock on that cold Saturday morning, it was still dark. The hacks had left the stand an hour and a half earlier. An article in the *Leader* recounted that the neighborhood beat cop and the private watchman checked the furrier's door several times during the night because they knew of the valuable stock inside. The last time they checked, it was six o'clock in the morning—the end of their shifts—and it was locked tight. About an hour later, the first employee of the day showed up and found the door open. Upon entering the store, he saw a pile of sealskin coats in the middle of the floor. The forms, racks and hooks in the display cases had been stripped of the most valuable sealskin coats, cloaks, dolmans and ulsters. The employee immediately called the police.

Cleveland detectives examined the door through which the burglars had gained entry. The thieves had drilled a five-eighths-inch hole halfway

Benedict & Ruedy's became Benedict & Mueller Furriers and moved from Superior Street to Euclid Avenue. *Cleveland Public Library.*

through the door and then inserted a three-eighths-inch bit to break all the way through. There was a long mark on the frame, and police thought that was how the burglars found the right point to bore their hole in the door. They then used a screw punch to force the catch open, even though it was fastened by two long screws. There were also jimmy marks along the bottom of the door. Some of the burglary tools were found inside the store, and it was later discovered they had been stolen the night before from a carpentry shop on Erie.

It was obvious to police that the first thing the crooks did was attack the large iron safe, which stood in the center of the store. They used some type of bar to try to lift the door from the hinges. When they were unsuccessful, they tried drilling a hole in the door. When that did not work, they tried boring a hole in one of the hinge lugs. After that failed, they abandoned the safe for the furs. They loaded fifty-one fur garments weighing at least 275 pounds into a waiting carriage outside the door. Mr. Ruedy, one of the owners, estimated the loss at $7,000.

As the day wore on, witnesses stepped forward with stories of unusual activities in the neighborhood. A carriage had been seen around 6:35 that morning driving rapidly up Superior. An American Express driver said that at 6:20, he had seen two men with their arms full of what looked like coats. They turned off Ontario and walked up St. Clair, he said.

Some of the policemen thought from the marks on the door that the burglars were unskilled. One of the detectives thought differently. "Think of men going into the store and robbing it of such property with a policeman standing on the corner not two hundred feet away," he told a *Leader* reporter after police had developed a few clues. "They are clever thieves and slick ones. You can't put sealskin coats in a snuff box as you can diamonds, and yet three rascals loaded fifty-one of them into a carriage and drove off without detection."

The thieves had carried the coats to a boardinghouse on St. Clair where they had rented a room three weeks prior to the robbery. The landlady said they were prompt with their rent money. She was not suspicious of them until they disappeared and she read about the robbery.

The thieving trio quickly packed the skins into two Saratoga trunks and smuggled them out a back window. The plan was to load the trunks onto Thomas Storey's wagon, stationed behind the Tabernacle, and drive them to the Bedford train station. Time was short, and Bedford was twelve miles away. Storey would have to run his horse hard in order to make the train bound for Pittsburgh. Halfway there, his horse became exhausted, so he stole a horse from a farmer's barn and left his own behind. He made it to the station with six minutes to spare and loaded the trunks onto the platform.

On Storey's trip home, he collected his horse and turned the other animal loose in the farmer's field. On the road, he was stopped by a Newburg policeman, Joe Whittaker, who was suspicious of his actions. Storey claimed to have delivered a load of furniture to a house near the Ohio Insane Asylum. Although Whittaker did not believe him, he let him go. Storey was arrested a few days later and questioned by Cleveland Police Captain Henry Hoehn. While in custody, he broke down and furnished a description of the men who had given him the trunks. When police searched his barn, they found a large cotton cover. Mr. Ruedy identified it as one they used at the store to keep dust off the goods. Storey was held for $1,500 bail.

Police Superintendent Jacob W. Schmitt sent telegraphs to all the large cities about the robbery. The Albany, New York police chief telegraphed back that from the burglars' methods, it sounded like a gang that he had sent to jail two years before. The men did eighteen months for an attempted fur store burglary in Albany and had been released in September. The chief sent a picture of one of the men and detailed descriptions of the others. They matched with what Cleveland police had been able to gather.

Captain Henry Hoehn became Cleveland's police superintendent in 1893 and served for three years. *Cleveland Police Historical Society Inc.*

Next, police discovered that Louis Myers was the conductor of the train that carried the two trunks. They asked him if he had seen anyone fitting the descriptions who came from Albany. One of the thieves was five-foot-ten and weighed about 160 pounds. He had dark hair and a smooth face. The other was five-foot-five and heavyset. He had a large, thick moustache, and his face was pockmarked. Myers said he did remember the men. The taller one was wearing a dark suit and overcoat and a stiff hat. The second man also wore dark clothes and a stiff hat. Furthermore, Myers remembered their tickets were for Allegheny City.

With this information, Superintendent Schmitt sent lengthy telegraphs to both Allegheny City and Pittsburgh. He also decided to send one of the department's most capable detectives, Captain Henry Hoehn, to work with Pittsburgh police on the case. Hoehn left on the 11:00 p.m. train on Monday, January 31.

Within two days, Hoehn telegraphed back to Schmitt that he and Pittsburgh police had arrested Harry "Kid" McMunn as one of the burglars but that the skins were nowhere to be found. Hoehn was afraid the goods had been sent out east. Schmitt telegraphed the larger eastern city police departments to keep an eye out for the burglars and the sealskin garments. Hoehn and Pittsburgh Detective Willis found out about a house where the burglars had taken a room. When the detectives got there, the room was deserted except for an empty trunk. The furs had been there but were now gone.

The woman in charge of the house said that two strangers had taken the room for a short time. The trunks were with them at that time, but several hours later, the men left with one of them. As near as Hoehn and Willis

Blinky Morgan made his move at the Pennsylvania Railroad Station in Ravenna, built in 1875. *Private collection of Thomas G. Gregory.*

could tell, the trunk had been taken to the Union Depot, but after that, there was no trace of it.

Detective William Hulligan was assigned to obtain requisition papers in order to bring McMunn back to Cleveland. He then took a train to Pittsburgh to assist in bringing the prisoner back. At midnight on February 4, Hulligan and Hoehn boarded the Cleveland & Pittsburgh train with McMunn handcuffed to Hulligan.

It was two o'clock in the morning when the train stopped at Alliance. Blinky Morgan, James Robinson and John Coughlin boarded the platform behind the smoker in which the detectives and their prisoner were riding. Morgan was wearing an old, faded beaver overcoat. One of the three was carrying a package wrapped in newspaper. Another of the trio passed through the smoker and looked around as if to see the "lay of the land" and then joined the other two. Hoehn was suspicious of the three from the start.

At about four o'clock in the morning, the train reached the Ravenna station and stopped there for a few minutes. Ten people were in the coach, including the two police officers and their prisoner. Two of the men who had boarded at Alliance rose from their seats and started for the door, but they abruptly stopped in front of Hulligan and McMunn. Suddenly, one of them struck Captain Hoehn on the head. He jumped to his feet and tried to grab the man by the neck, but he was turned around. From his description, the man—most likely Blinky Morgan—was older. His moustache was sprinkled with grey, and he had a week's growth of beard. There was a bald spot at the back of his head. He bit Hoehn's finger so hard that the policeman cried out in pain.

Hulligan had been hit squarely in the head with a coupling pin wrapped in newspaper. During the scuffle with Hoehn, the outlaw said in a low voice, "Goddamn, he is getting the best of me."

At that, another man whirled toward Hoehn. He hit the captain with the coupling pin, and Hoehn sank down into the seat. He was bleeding badly but trying to get back on his feet and still grappling with his attacker. As he rose from the floor, he yanked his gun out of the holster and began firing toward the clump of men surrounding his partner, Hulligan. At least one of the men fired back, hitting him twice in the right arm and once near the ribs. The man he had been fighting with pointed a gun at him. Hoehn threw up both his hands and cried out, "Oh my God! Is there no help?" The man fired, hitting him in the hip.

The other people in the car crawled down behind the seats when the bullets started to fly. A minister from Cleveland pulled his bag over his head and stuffed himself under his seat.

Unconscious and still shackled to McMunn, Hulligan was dragged out of the train and onto the platform, where Morgan and his men rifled his pockets for the keys to the handcuffs. Once McMunn was free, he, Morgan, Robinson and Coughlin escaped into the dark.

Some believe Morgan was wounded and that he fled to Pittsburgh, where his girlfriend, Nellie Lowery, Coughlin's sister, extracted the bullets and nursed him back to health. However, one newspaper reported that after his death, the coroners found no evidence of him ever being shot.

Nellie had quite the back story. She was married to Charles Lowery, one of Morgan's gang members. When her husband was in jail, however, she took up with Morgan. There was also evidence that she ran a brothel in Cleveland.

The two policemen were taken back to Cleveland. Hulligan died four days later at his home with his wife and five children at his bedside. Hoehn was taken to City Hospital, where he recuperated from his wounds.

Even though there was a $16,000 reward offered for the capture of Charles "Blinky" Morgan, Harry "Kid" McMunn, James Robinson and John Coughlin, there was not a trace of the murderous outlaws. Lawmen throughout the region hunted the men for five months.

During the time Morgan was being hunted, stories surfaced of past daring prisons breaks and an alliance with the James-Younger Gang. McMunn was

Cleveland Police Department's wanted poster for some of Morgan's gang members. Matthew Kennedy was also known as Harry "Kid" McMunn. *Cleveland Police Historical Society Inc.*

with him during a Michigan escape. He left a note behind telling the warden he would have stayed if the food weren't so bad. He and McMunn were doing time for breaking into a post office in Grand Rapids.

Finally, in June, police got a break by way of a little boy who told a friend that his "Uncle" Charles Morgan was staying at his house in Alpena, Michigan. The boy's mother, Mrs. Frank D. Williams, had rented rooms to Morgan, Robinson and Coughlin. McMunn had disappeared.

The woman may have been Nellie Lowery. The three men had seemed suspicious to the people of the small town. Alpena Deputy George Jones went undercover to watch the three men, although he did not know who they were at this point. Morgan acted strangely, as if he would shoot anybody if provoked. He went out only under cover of night and always with a gun in his hand. Jones said the other hand was in a sling.

Alpena County Sheriff Charles C. Lynch contacted Cleveland authorities with descriptions of the three and received back a warrant to arrest the men. Henry Hoehn was back on his feet, so he and Detective John "Jack" Reeves started up the lake to Alpena. But before they got there, Lynch, Deputy J.E. Denton and City Marshal Westrop made their move. Lynch was aware that the suspects were about to leave the area. On June 27, he and Westrop took Robinson and Coughlin by surprise just as they were about to board a boat, *The City of Mackinaw*, to Oscoda, Michigan. The apprehension went without a fight, and the two men were lodged in the county jail. Then Sheriff Lynch and the arrest party set off to find Charles "Blinky" Morgan.

Lynch and his deputies went to the Williamses' house around 9:30 in the evening. They found Morgan in the sitting room reading a book. Mrs.

Williams was also in the room. She became flustered and introduced Morgan as her brother-in-law. As soon as Morgan saw the lawmen, he plunged his right hand into his pocket for his gun. Sheriff Lynch grabbed his throat and forced him down onto the floor. Morgan was on his back but managed to fire his .44-caliber gun a couple times. One of those bullets hit the sheriff in the leg. The woman screamed and ran from the room. Lynch held onto his neck. One of the deputies grabbed the gun. Finally, Morgan hollered, "I give up!"

The deputies subdued the outlaw and carted him off to jail. He gave a false name and threatened that the deputies would pay for arresting him.

Sheriff Lynch was taken to a sanitarium in Detroit, where he died on August 17 of blood poisoning from his wound. He was a popular and capable lawman just thirty-seven years old when he died.

Captain Hoehn and Detective Reeves took custody of Morgan and his confederates and brought them back to Cleveland on Friday, July 1, by boat. Hoehn noticed that Morgan had dyed his hair and moustache black.

An hour before the boat was to arrive, people started gathering at the dock. By the time the boat tied up, there were close to two thousand people waiting to see the criminals. A large detail of police was deployed to keep the crowd back. Two patrol wagons stood waiting at the landing.

Captain Hoehn came off the boat first to make sure everything was ready. He then went back on board, and a few minutes later, Morgan, Robinson and Coughlin were marched off the boat. They were surrounded by several detectives. Chained together, the three had their hands fastened with steel bands and were hustled into one of the patrol wagons.

A voice from the dock called out, "Hang them!" Morgan turned to see where the voice came from. The other two pulled their hats down over their eyes.

Detective William Hulligan's two sons were in the crowd.

A few days later, the outlaws were taken to Ravenna, where they would stand trial. They were lodged in the small, stone building that served as the Portage County Jail. It had six cells on the ground floor and six cells on a second tier that could be reached by an iron balcony. The three prisoners were allowed out of their cells for a few hours a day, but only one was allowed out at a time. Morgan was watched closely. A guard sat within a few feet of him at all times, and other deputies were stationed at the doors of the jail.

When Morgan got the news of Lynch's impending death, the *Summit County Beacon* revealed his reaction: "Well, God damn it, who wouldn't have shot him? How could I know who the men were who were surrounding me and attacking me? They could have been robbers for aught I knew. Any sane man would have protected himself as I did."

Another newspaper circulated in the jail gave an update on Lynch's condition. "There's that piece about Lynch, if ye want to read it, Charley."

Morgan grabbed the paper from the other prisoner's hand and turned toward his cell. "I'll read it inside—not here."

When the Michigan sheriff died, it was a guard who broke the news to Morgan. The old criminal was having a smoke outside his cell, it being his hour for exercise. "Is that so?" he said flatly and walked back into his cell. The guard noted that Morgan's face grew pale.

The October issues of the *Plain Dealer* and *Cleveland Leader* reported the happenings in the trial each day. Judge J.R. Johnston was on the bench. Portage County prosecutors E.W. Maxson and Isaac T. Siddall presented the state's case, and Sam Eddy and John McSweeney defended Morgan.

When jury selection was finished, the heart of the trial—the testimony—began and caused quite a sensation. It drew spectators from Akron, Cleveland, Youngstown and Pittsburgh. The biggest part of the crowd was made up of women, and Morgan seemed to appreciate their attention. He was fifty-three years old, but he held himself erect with perfect posture and wore a white tie. As he was led into court each day, he would nod at the press. At times, he tipped his chair onto its back legs and rocked.

The prosecution claimed it would bring thirty witnesses to the stand. Its first order of business was to connect Morgan to the burglary of Benedict & Ruedy's Hatter and Furriers. Sam Eddy objected to nearly every question Maxson asked of his witnesses, claiming that any testimony in regard to the stolen furs in no way showed that his client was on that train in Ravenna when Detective Hulligan was killed. The judge overruled Eddy.

Eddy also objected when Dr. Michael Lavell, the warden of the Kingston, Ontario penitentiary, was called to the stand. He said that Morgan had been incarcerated in his prison and so had Matthew Kennedy, aka Harry "Kid" McMunn. He said Morgan's past record might "blacken the character of Morgan by showing he had been in the penitentiary."

According to the *Plain Dealer*, McSweeney argued, "I know very well that testimony showing that Morgan was in the penitentiary simply would be lighter than stuff dreams are made of, but it was wanted to show the close relationship between Morgan and McMunn." He went on to say the testimony would show the two had been partners in crime and escaped from that penitentiary together. He said it would show why Morgan was willing to risk his life and shed other men's blood in such a dangerous rescue attempt.

The judge denied the objection and allowed the jury to hear the testimony.

One night after court, four women from Akron followed Morgan and Sheriff Sheldon to the jail to get another look at the prisoner. Sheldon denied them. He would allow no one access to the alleged murderer, not even Nellie Lowery.

The most intense part of the trial came when the prosecution started calling people to the stand who had been on the train the night Hulligan was bludgeoned to death.

The conductor of the fateful train, Louis Ohliger, told the jury he had taken tickets from Morgan, Robinson and Coughlin at Alliance and had seen them board the train and take seats in the smoking car. "They sat in different places in the car; from one end to the other," he said.

He described one of the men, Morgan, as having "heavy eyebrows, rather bushy hair, and he was probably fifty years old. I saw that he was a bit bald. I was behind him, and when he raised his hat, I saw." He identified Morgan in the courtroom.

At Ravenna, Ohliger was getting off the train when he heard something that sounded like a row. "I was on my way to the smoking car when I was met by a man with a revolver," he said. "I did not understand what was going on, so I tried to move forward. The man then fired a shot but did not hit me." He then ran back to the baggage car and "got something purporting to be a shooting iron." He ran back to the end of the smoking car and tried to cock the gun, but first he ran into a man with a revolver who threatened him to get out. The lights were out in the car, but he saw the "scuffling." He then ran to one of the other coaches, pulled the bell rope, jumped off the train and ran back to the station, where he saw Hulligan sitting in a seat. The detective was stooped over and bleeding, and there was an empty handcuff hanging from his wrist. As the conductor looked up, he saw four men running down the track. He went back onto the train and saw pools of blood where Hulligan and Hoehn had been attacked. "Blood was spattered around the car," he said, "and there were several bullet holes in different places."

Passenger Joseph Rauch of Bellevue was riding in the coach next to the smoking car and remembered the three men getting on the train at Alliance. He noticed one in particular. His description was the same as the conductor's, and he identified Morgan at the defense table. "I heard scuffling and shots fired," testified Rauch, "and I heard someone say, 'Get away from there.'"

John G. Watts, a carpenter from Bristol, Indiana, who had also been riding on the train, was sworn in. He testified:

Four men came into the car when it stopped at Ravenna. I thought one had a newspaper in his hand. He struck Captain Hoehn at the same time another man struck Detective Hulligan. Captain Hoehn was struck half a dozen blows. He dropped to his knees between the seats. The other man was striking the detective, and he got at least a half dozen blows...I saw the blood stream down over his face, and he was senseless. I heard Captain Hoehn call for help: "Can't you help me?" I heard Hulligan groan three or four times as if in misery.

Watts thought there were as many as ten or twelve shots fired. The lights were out, and he did not see Hoehn from when he was knocked down until it was over. "I got down between the seats, as the bullets were pretty thick. I saw three or four men dragging Hulligan out."

When asked to identify the man who delivered the blows to Hulligan and Hoehn, Watts pointed out Blinky Morgan. "He resembles him very closely."

Watts did not get as good of a look at the other men. He said Hoehn was the first to fire. "As soon as he shot once, or perhaps twice, the others began to fire. About that time, the lights went out, except for one in the front of the car, and I couldn't see anything after that."

McSweeney asked what Captain Hoehn did when he was struck.

"He put his hand up," said Watts. "He was hit on the side of the head first, and then he was struck again and again until he dropped down. The other men were striking Hulligan at the same time, and when Captain Hoehn was down, his assailant went to them." They demanded the key from Hulligan, who told them he didn't have it. One of the men watching the door shouted, "Bring out your man!"

Twenty-year-old Nellie Campbell, alias Kennedy, was a passenger on the train that night. She slept during part of the trip, and when she awoke, there was a man sitting behind her. She asked him if he knew where she could get water. He was kind enough to get the water for her. "When he came back, I looked up in his face and thanked him," she said. "He wore a faded heavy overcoat, a heavy cap pulled down over his eyes, [and] a moustache long at the ends but trimmed near the lips. At Ravenna, I saw him again on the platform. I got up and went to the door, but he held a revolver at me and said, 'Stand back there or I'll kill you!' He shot two or three times, and I heard him say, 'Get your man out there. My shots are nearly all gone! Get your man out!' Then I saw men drag somebody out of the car." When asked if she could point out the man, she indicated Morgan. "There he is," she said. "The one with the glasses and the white tie."

Sam Eddy immediately went to work to discredit her, and the *Plain Dealer* reported his line of questioning. "What condition were you in when you got on the train at Pittsburgh as far as intoxication is concerned?" Eddy asked. "Were you intoxicated?"

"Had a bottle of whiskey with you, didn't you? Didn't you and Maude Smith have whiskey with you?" he asked, referring to a friend who was traveling with her.

The young woman denied his accusations.

"You are in the habit of getting intoxicated?"

"Sometimes."

Eddy then managed to elicit that she had been in the workhouse in Cleveland for four weeks for "disturbance." And before that, she had done a shorter stint in the workhouse and had several fines in the police courts of Cleveland and Pittsburgh.

When she left Cleveland, she went to Youngstown. "Were you arrested there?" he asked.

"Yes, sir."

Cleveland detective Jack Reeves brought Nellie back to Cleveland for the trial, and Eddy tried to get her to say the policeman had paid her, which she stoutly denied.

The next witness was Reverend Carl Weiss of Cleveland. He had ridden in the smoking car on the same side as Hoehn, Hulligan and the prisoner. He was asked what took place after the train stopped at Ravenna.

"A few men passed me by. One had a fur cap on, and he, with three or four others, acted as if they were going out of the car. The man with a fur cap had a folded newspaper in his hand, and he struck Captain Hoehn on the head. At the same time another man hit Detective Hulligan. He jumped up and fell over. Captain Hoehn also jumped up and grappled with the large man."

The minister and one of the deputies then illustrated the struggle for the jury. "They were pounding at Hulligan at the same time," he said. "Someone called for help, and the man struggling with Hoehn cried 'He's getting the best of me.'"

Weiss said another man came from the rear of the car, with a gun in each hand aimed at his face, and said, "Move, and I'll kill you." He testified that the men hit Hulligan eight or nine times, telling him to unlock the handcuffs, but he was unable. He heard someone say, "Kill him! Drag him out! Get your man out!" Weiss also pointed to Blinky Morgan in the courtroom.

Nellie Lowery and several more of Morgan's friends sat in the row behind him at trial. During recess, Morgan turned and extended his hand to Nellie. She hesitated but grabbed it and then kissed him.

On the day Captain Henry Hoehn came to the stand, the courtroom was filled to capacity. The overflow waited in the hallways, and when a seat opened up in the courtroom, the deputies would allow someone in the hall to take that seat.

The prosecutor took Hoehn back over his ordeal, and it was reported in vivid detail in the *Leader* and the *Plain Dealer*. "All of a sudden, I was struck on the side and back of the head," Captain Hoehn said. "I rose to my feet and grabbed a man around the neck, but I was turned around. I got a hold of his moustache with my right hand. He got my second finger in his mouth and bit me terribly. It gave me intense pain, worse than when I was struck." And at this time, Hoehn heard Hulligan "give a most heart-rending groan, and that was the last I heard poor Hulligan say."

At this, Fannie Hulligan, the detective's widow, who was in the courtroom, burst out in sobs.

During the scuffle, Hoehn then reached out with his left hand and clutched the older man's throat. "God damn, he is getting the best of me," the outlaw said in a low voice.

At that, one of the other men whirled toward the policeman. "He had something in his hand wrapped in paper," testified Hoehn. "It was about eight or ten inches long. He held it in both hands…then all at once, whatever it was came down on my forehead where this scar is." Hoehn pointed to his forehead.

Hoehn said he felt himself sink down into the seat, but the next thing he knew, he was back on his feet again, still grappling with the man. "He got me to the end of the car and down on the floor. I was bleeding pretty freely."

Trying to rise up from the floor, he yanked his gun out of the holster and began firing at the clump of men surrounding Hulligan. At least one of the men fired back, hitting him twice in the right arm and once near the ribs.

He looked up and saw the old man standing above him. He was bracing himself with one of the seats. "With his right hand, he leveled his revolver at me." Hoehn was out of bullets, so he turned away. "It was then that the man fired the shot that went into my hip."

"Look around the room," Maxson said, "and see if you can pick out that man."

"Yes sir, I see him sitting there with the spectacles on."

"You mean Morgan?"

"Yes, I mean Morgan."

Morgan's defense in the case was strange in that there was no defense. No one came to the witness stand to testify on his behalf, and no alibi was offered. Even more bizarre was that Eddy offered no closing argument.

The jury had been sequestered during the entire trial. Two deputies were assigned to watch them day and night. All of their sleeping cots were set up in one hotel room, and they ate all their meals with a deputy sheriff at each end of the table. Every night after dinner, the jurors were allowed a walk under the watchful eye of the deputies. After the day's testimony, they were taken to a special room where they waited until the crowds had cleared before they left the courthouse.

After closing arguments and the jury charge, the jurors retired to deliberate. They came back with their verdict in less than an hour and a half: guilty.

Morgan was sentenced to hang on March 16, 1888, but an appeal to the Circuit Court, which claimed an error by allowing testimony of the fur store robbery and Morgan's past criminal history to enter into the record, pushed the date back to June 1. The appeal was turned down. Governor J.B. Foraker extended the date to August 3, 1888.

Charles "Blinky" Morgan went to his death proclaiming his innocence. The newspapers said he looked like a "high-toned gentlemen dressed for an evening ball" in a well-fitting black suit with a standing collar, a white cravat and a buttonhole bouquet. He had asked that Detective Reeves and three other Cleveland policemen not be admitted to see him executed. Instead, he asked for a friend, Jimmy Maguire, to be there. Warden Coffin said he would comply

The "Beau Brummel" of the police department, Detective John "Jack" Reeves helped bring in Morgan and attended the hanging. *Cleveland Police Historical Society Inc.*

with Morgan's final wishes, but Reeves and the other lawmen entered the room anyway. When Maguire saw them, he protested against the "presence of these murderers." Coffin told Maguire to keep still or go out of the room. He said the policemen had to go out, too. Maguire left. Morgan quietly asked for him to come back. "No, I prefer to go. I don't want to see this," he said.

The last thing Morgan saw before the hood was drawn over his face was Detective Jack Reeves and the other policemen looking at him.

"Good-bye, Nellie," Morgan said, and at 1:22 a.m., the trap was pulled. He dropped seven feet into hell. The fall did not break his neck. Instead, it took twenty-four grisly minutes of him fighting and writhing for the rope to strangle him to death. The doctors held his arms and feet until his heart quit beating.

Charles "Blinky" Morgan was one of the last men to be hanged in the state of Ohio. His body was turned over to Nellie Lowery, and he was buried in Columbus.

James Robinson and John Coughlin were tried and found guilty but granted new trials. They never came before a judge again because the evidence was lacking. Coughlin died sometime later, and Robinson went back to Pittsburgh, where he became a respectable shoe merchant.

Harry "Kid" McMunn, aka Matthew Kennedy, was arrested for burglary out in Colorado, but the jail could not hold him. He was captured in Chicago, sent back to Colorado and escaped again. No one knows for sure where he landed. Some said England. Some said Paris. Still others said Australia. Or maybe it was Mexico.

Captain Henry Hoehn had joined the force in 1866 as a patrolman and rose in the ranks to the top spot. He was appointed superintendent of the Cleveland Police Department on July 1, 1893, and served for three years. He died suddenly in 1903.

The furs were never recovered.

CHAPTER 4
SHOT DOWN IN COLD BLOOD

It was pitch-dark out on Friday night, June 8, 1888, when Joe Ketchum was gunned down on a Big Four train near the Ohio River.

The first to tell the story of what happened to the brave baggage master was Henry J. Zimmerman, the American Express messenger. He and Ketchum were riding alone in the combination baggage-express car aboard the Cincinnati, Indianapolis, St. Louis & Chicago (Big Four) train headed for Cincinnati. It was around ten o'clock and the locomotive had just pulled out of Delhi, twelve miles east of Cincinnati, when Zimmerman spotted some tramps through the glass window of the car's front door. "Joe, there's somebody at the front end of the car," he said.

The baggage master looked up and saw tramps standing out on the platform next to the tender. It was dark, but he could see that there were four of them, and they were wearing black masks.

Ketchum was known for his good nature, but he did not take kindly to tramps riding on the train for free. If he caught them, the large forty-year-old would throw them off. So when he saw these men, he grabbed his lantern and got up to go to the door. He got only a few feet before the intruders opened fire with a volley of fifteen pieces of lead. Shards of glass sprayed the car, and six bullets ripped into Ketchum's abdomen and neck. He collapsed just short of the door.

Zimmerman, who escaped without injury, spoke with an unnamed *Cincinnati Commercial Tribune* reporter who was first on the scene when the train pulled into Central Station after the shooting.

The express agent claimed he tried to draw his pistol but that it caught on his hip pocket, and he could not get it out. Then he ran to the rear platform, "keeping low" as the tramps burst through the door. Zimmerman hightailed it to the smoker, where Conductor William Lefler was riding. According to the reporter, the conductor was a veteran and known to be calm under pressure.

Lefler said Zimmerman flew into the smoking car and shouted that a gang was robbing the train. Having heard shots coming from the baggage car, Lefler was already on his feet. He was not armed, so he ran back into the next coach and announced to the passengers that he needed a revolver. Only one man presented himself to the conductor. The two started forward. "I thought the best thing to do then was to stop the train, so I gave the signal to the engine on the bell rope," said Lefler. But the train did not stop, which surprised him. It was not until later that he learned the engineer and fireman had problems of their own.

Lefler and two or three other men went up to the baggage car. "As I opened the door, I saw three men just going out the door at the forward end of the car," said Lefler. They were rifling through the wounded man's pockets, he said, and reloading their guns. "They were getting out as quick as they could." Their exit was so fast that the conductor could not see their faces; he could see only that they wore dark clothing and hats slouched down over their faces. "They looked like tramps," he said. "Their clothing was rough."

Lefler kept making signals to stop the train. Finally, he put on the automatic brakes, and the locomotive slowed to a crawl and then stopped around Trautman. He thought the robbers left the train at that point. When the train finally came to a halt, he charged up to the engine and found out that his engineer had been attacked and had not been able to stop the train.

"Joe Ketchum made a gallant fight," the conductor said. "His lamp, which I saw, was all smashed, and the wires were bent where it had struck the robber's head." He told the reporter that the baggage master had a reputation up and down the track of being a brave man. "The robbers may not have known this, but they quickly found out."

"Zimmerman," Lefler said, "ran out of the car as soon as the firing commenced, and poor Ketchum was left alone."

The engineer, an old soldier named James Boyd, had been at the throttle of Engine No. 35 for sixteen years. "We left Delhi on time, and after I pulled away from the station I started her up lively," he told reporters who had begun to gather at Central Station. When the train was a short way out from Delhi, he heard a shot toward the rear of the engine. "I didn't know it was a shot; I kind of thought it was a torpedo, and I looked back and saw a flash. It was then that I saw the robbers. There were three of them. They were on the front platform of the baggage car, and they fired through the window."

It was dark, but he could see the form of a man in the lantern light coming toward him. "One of them climbed over the tank of the tender, revolver in hand, and came at me over the coal." It happened so fast, Boyd said, that he was paralyzed for a few seconds. "When he got close to the engine, he pointed the revolver at me. I dropped the throttle, threw up the lid of my toolbox and, reaching down, got hold of a monkey wrench. I resolved to sell my life as dearly as possible."

The scoundrel dropped down to the narrow place between the engine and tender and shouted, "Throw up your hands!"

The engineer refused.

The robber pulled the trigger, but the gun did not fire. Boyd knew then it was going to be an all-out fight, and he was ready with the heavy tool in his hand. "I didn't soldier for years to be afraid of one man."

At first sight, Boyd thought the intruders were just tramps and would not be much inclined to fight. But when he saw the one fellow with a gun in his hand, he knew they were robbers and he was in for a tussle.

The two came together on the floorboard of No. 35 between the tender and locomotive. "When he got near, I jumped at him and struck him with the wrench," said Boyd. The robber was on guard and deflected the blow. "I knew the gun would not go off because he kept pulling the trigger and there was no report. I finally gave him a good blow with the monkey wrench, and he dropped to the platform." Boyd then got a good grip on the gun and yanked it away from him. All during the fight, the train was "banging away at a lively rate." "Nobody was at the throttle," the former soldier said.

Boyd got the gun away from the robber and beat him with the butt end of it. "I gave him some pretty hard blows, but he fought like the devil."

Just then, Fireman Henry Fisher waded into the struggle, but the space was so small that Boyd was afraid the wrong person might tumble from the train. Boyd had the upper hand, but he was a small, compact man, and he was afraid his adversary was stronger than he was. The robber wrestled the gun back from Boyd, but Boyd got it away again. "The fireman then took a hand. I was fighting the fellow for all I was worth. I tried to kill him," said Boyd.

The robber weakened. "Don't kill me," he cried. "I'm only a boy. I didn't intend to get into this, and I won't do it again."

"No!" Boyd exclaimed. "You won't do it again." The engineer was weakening, and the robber was trying to force him over the edge of the engine. "Then I tried to back him over the coal. He raised up with me, and I got him by the throat."

Right then, Fisher yelled, "Here comes another fellow!"

Boyd looked up and saw a second man trying to climb over the coal, shouting, "Wait a minute, Joe. We are coming!"

"My fireman jumped to the throttle, pulled her open and away she went," Boyd said. "The two fellows jumped or fell off into the ditch." The direction of their flight was a mystery. "My fireman then came to my assistance, and we got hold of the robber together and pitched him off the engine head over heels. We were running then, I guess about eighteen miles an hour."

"You bet he was a strong one," the engineer added.

According to Boyd and Fisher, the assailant had the smooth face of a boy, and his hair was short. "I know it was short because I couldn't get a grip on it. He was dark-skinned or else sunburnt [*sic*]."

During the fight, the robber's hat fell off and got left behind when he was ejected from the train. It was a worn-out, brown Derby-style hat with grease on it. The lining was gone, but the label that read "United Hatters of North America" was still sewn inside.

Fireman Henry Fisher was a young man and obviously excited when he talked to the newspaper at the station in Cincinnati. "I looked after the engine while the engineer was fighting this fellow," he said. "I thought the best thing to do was look after the engine and try to stop the train." When it looked like Boyd might lose the battle, Fisher left the throttle to help. "Jim banged him with a monkey wrench first, and then they fought over the revolver. It was a hot fight. I helped all I could, but I was looking ahead."

In a later interview with the papers, Boyd gave Fisher no credit for helping him. "He seemed powerless from fright and was incapable of offering any assistance," he said of the fireman.

Fisher said the two robbers he saw wore slouch hats and had "something" over their faces.

Boyd said, "I think I would know the man who was on my engine if I should meet him in California, as his features were indelibly imprinted on my mind."

Boyd said had he known what happened to Ketchum, he would not have let the robber go. He later boasted that he could have easily held him, as he had him at his mercy. He also later claimed that he alone had "raised the fellow up and pitched him bodily from the engine."

The bandits got away with murder but bungled the robbery. The train was carrying an express safe, but according to the papers, there was not much in it. If the engineer and fireman had not put up such a fight, the villains would have taken over the train and robbed the forty some passengers, all of whom were "of the better class" and undoubtedly were carrying cash and wearing valuable watches and jewelry.

The scene at Cincinnati Central Station was chaos, with swarms of railroad men, citizens and reporters. By midnight, a train with at least thirty Cincinnati lawmen left for Delhi hoping to enlist the help of police there. The police anticipated finding the streets of Delhi full of citizens who were outraged over the assault on the Big Four train. Instead, they found the town dark and the streets deserted. Even the Big Four station was quiet. Chief Gill, who led the party, had to wake up the Delhi constable. The constable had not heard what happened, but he quickly jumped out of bed, dressed and joined the hunt.

In Hamilton County, the sheriff formed a posse of men both on horseback and on foot and set out to scour the riverfront by lantern light. They were joined by a large number of armed citizens.

During the search, the police talked with four farmers who, on their way to market, had a run-in with four masked highwaymen on the Delhi pike, not far from the town of Delhi. They described the robbers as "big, stout, young fellows" with guns that they "flourished around freely."

One of the farmers took off after the assailants. He followed them until he saw them jump in a skiff and row out into the river. All the robbers got from the farmers was a mere five cents.

Depot at Delhi, circa 1960s. *Society of Historic Sharonville.*

Kentucky authorities were notified to be on the lookout because skiffs were numerous along the Ohio River banks, especially in the area of the robbery, and some felt there was a possibility the robbers took to the water and disappeared up into the Kentucky hills.

Henry Zimmerman told authorities he thought the men were expert robbers because they were steady and cool and had large-caliber guns.

Detectives collected the brass shells from the floor of the baggage car. They were for .40- and .44-caliber guns. Cincinnati Chief Detective Lawrence M. Hazen did not think the robbers were professional "because they made a poor choice of booty." Known as one of the thief takers, Larry Hazen felt the crime was committed by tramps, but other police insisted common tramps did not use that type of weapon. The gun that the engineer yanked from the hands of the one assailant was a large, navy-sized double-action pistol. Neither the gun nor the hat furnished any clues as to the identity of the robber.

Police felt that the man who climbed over the tender and got into the fight with the engineer was going to take control of the train. When he was foiled, the others jumped off.

Shortly before the Big Four train was attacked, shots were fired nearby at another accommodation train. More stories rolled in to authorities about "bad characters around Delhi," and police tracked down every lead they could.

Joe Ketchum was taken from the train at Central Station to his home at Mill Street. While four doctors—two from the railroad—worked feverishly to save his life, telegraphs sent word to his brothers and sisters. One report stated that he had been given whiskey and it made him sick. At eight o'clock the morning after the shooting, the doctors decided to try to remove the bullets from his head and abdomen. One bullet was extracted from the back of his neck near his right ear. Two more rounds were taken out of his lower abdomen. During the procedure, the doctors found that his bowel had a two-inch perforation. They knew then that his chance for survival was almost nonexistent. But he seemed to rest easier after that, maybe due to strong narcotics. There was a report at eleven o'clock that morning stating that he had died, but it was premature. Ketchum would live a few more hours.

The railroad manager, Mr. Green, called at the Ketchum home in the early afternoon. As he left the house, he told the physicians to spare no expense.

When M.E. Ingalls, the president of the Cincinnati, Indianapolis, St. Louis & Chicago Railroad, was notified of the incident, he immediately telegraphed from the New York office that the company was offering a "one thousand dollar reward for the arrest and conviction of the robbers." The offer was officially advertised in a column of the *Commercial Gazette*.

Ketchum's wife, Sallie (née Sarah A. Logan), stayed at his bedside. He told her he expected to die and did the best he could to console her. His eighty-two-year-old father, also named Joseph, three of his sisters (Phoebe Schofield of Greensburg, Indiana; Susan Dean of Milan, Indiana; and Isabella Barrows of Cincinnati) and two of his brothers, Ira and Benjamin Ketchum of Greensburg, were all able to get there in time to join the death vigil. His brother James and sister Rhoda were apparently not there.

Joseph W. Ketchum was born on September 14, 1847, in Cheviot, Ohio. He was the youngest of eight children. Most of his life was spent in Greensburg, Decatur County, Indiana. In 1870, he became a brakeman for the Big Four railroad, and two years later, he shifted positions to become a baggage master. During this period, he boarded in different houses in Cincinnati but kept his home in Indiana. Finally, in 1884, he and Sallie moved to Cincinnati.

By 4:30 p.m., Ketchum started to decline at an alarming rate. One of the physicians warned the family that he would not live another four hours. "His face had assumed the saffron hue of death," the doctor said. Ketchum was still conscious until the end when one of the women was fanning his sweaty brow. His last words were, "Fan me faster." Around five o'clock on the afternoon of June 9, he gasped two or three times and was gone.

The same doctors who had operated on Ketchum earlier in the day performed a postmortem. They found two more slugs, one imbedded next to his spine and another that had pierced his bladder. Either bullet could have caused death.

All of the trainmen at the Central Passenger Station—brakemen, conductors, firemen and engineers—were stunned and grieved. Ketchum had been well liked by the men he worked with. They said he was "a big, good-natured man without malice toward anyone, and he had no bad habits."

At 8:20 a.m. on June 10, Joe Ketchum's body left his home for the last time. He was taken to the Central Depot, where a special train awaited to carry his casket and his family, friends and train crew to Indiana.

When the funeral train pulled into the station at Greensburg, it was met by more than one hundred friends who had come to pay their respects.

To thirty-five-year-old Sallie Ketchum, the death of her husband must have been horrific. She had already suffered tragedy three times before. She and Joe had married in June 1879 and had three children. Sadly, all three babies—two girls and a boy—died before they were two months old. Her

Central Union Depot, 1905. *Cincinnati Museum Center.*

children were buried in little graves at South Park Cemetery in Greensburg, and she buried her husband beside them. Among the numerous floral tributes was one from his train associates; it was a baggage car with the name "Joe" on the side.

Authorities in Hamilton County were working every angle to find the killers but coming up empty-handed in the hunt. One posse of handpicked men headed up by a police sergeant scoured the tracks and riverbank near where Engineer James Boyd thought he and Fireman Henry Fisher had hurled the bandit from the moving train. Boyd felt surely the man was badly injured if not killed. The posse found two pools of blood below a fence near Monlton's Woods. It looked as though someone had leaned his head on the rail. Tracks led away from the spot and in the direction of the river. The police followed them but lost the trail in a deep ravine.

It seems as though Boyd was wrong about where he and Fisher tossed the blackguard. At about three o'clock on Saturday morning, Sam Finney, the one-legged toll collector at the gate opposite Rapid Run Creek, was awakened by police and questioned whether he had seen or heard anything. He remembered when the train passed his tollhouse, which stood on a ridge that overlooked the Big Four tracks, because he was sitting near his front door when the train passed. The train was "going at a pretty good clip," he said. A short time later, he heard someone about one hundred feet away climbing up the embankment from the tracks. He looked toward the sound and saw the form of a man running across the pike. "The fellow was on a dead run and kept up his pace until he disappeared up Rapid Run," recalled Finney. Finney did not know what had happened aboard the train, so he did not think a lot about it.

Police had no doubt that the man Finney saw was the robber thrown from the train. They figured he must not have been injured that badly if he was crawling up the embankment and running through the trees, and he must have been well acquainted with the locality.

After talking with Finney, detectives worked the areas near the river and the tracks. Chief Gill ordered the embankment and ravine searched. Nothing was found, but Gill was now certain that at least one of the robbers was from the neighborhood and knew exactly where the best escape route was.

Sam Bassitt, another toll collector in the area, found a mask hanging from a bush near where Boyd tossed the man from engine and where the blood was found. The mask was roughly made out of black muslin and looked like the eyeholes had been cut with a knife.

Cincinnati's superintendent of police, Phillip P. Deitsch, sent telegrams with what descriptions police could gather to all the railroad detectives and law enforcement agencies along the track. He made a guess that one of the robbers might be James Anderson, who was a notorious burglar known to operate in the area.

Chief of Detectives Hazen thought the gang might be shell-workers or skin gamblers who had been operating in the vicinity. Having worked for Adams Express at one time, he had experience with all types of thieves and knew of instances where they had been thrown off Big Four trains. He also thought they could be drunken tramps desperate for money.

At 11:00 a.m. on Saturday, word came from the town of Cochran, just over the Indiana line, that four suspicious characters—most assuredly the guilty parties—were being held there. Several police detectives headed up by Larry Hazen, as well as newspaper reporters, set off for Cochran. They rode on a special train made up of Big Four Engine No. 14 and one coach, in which they would take the four men into custody.

The journey produced poor results, however. When their train arrived at Cochran, the detectives found that no one at the station knew anything about the prisoners. Hazen and his men were directed to the Aurora jail, where

Cincinnati police superintendents. *From left to right*: Thomas Duffy, George Hadley, Phillip Deitsch and Chief Lawrence Hazen. *Greater Cincinnati Police Historical Society Museum.*

they found the cell door open. A bystander volunteered the information that the prisoners had been taken before the magistrate. When they got to court, they found out that the magistrate had found no reason to detain the men, so he let them go.

At this point, Chief Hazen had lost his patience and was on his way back to the train when one of the suspects approached him. Hazen asked him his whereabouts in the days leading up to his arrest. The fellow gave a full accounting of his time, including a night spent in Cincinnati before the murder. He swore he had not been on Joe Ketchum's train and was willing to go back to Cincinnati and cooperate with their investigation. Hazen was apparently satisfied with his explanation, because he declined to take him back to Cincinnati.

On the way back to Cincinnati, the train made a stop at Lawrenceburg. The policemen and newsmen were confronted with a raucous throng of curiosity seekers. Threats of lynching rippled through the crowd. One woman offered to lead a mob to string up the prisoners, and police could not convince her that there were no prisoners on the train. Later, they found out she was a Big Four engineer's wife and a lifelong friend of Joe Ketchum.

A mass of people awaited Hazen and his entourage when the train pulled back into Grand Central Depot. When no prisoners were unloaded, the crowd was disappointed and started to disperse. It seems as though the murder had riled everyone.

Citizens living for miles along the railroad track took up arms and began search expeditions. The $1,000 reward did not have as much effect on people as the cry for revenge. Had the culprits been found, they most certainly would have been lynched.

The day after the funeral, the *Cincinnati Enquirer* reported the story of a number of desperados holed up in an old abandoned house in a thicket three miles from Delhi. Early on Monday evening, June 11, twelve lawmen under the direction of Chief Gill and Lieutenant Schmidt surrounded the house located on the Muddy Creek only a mile from where the attempted robbery had occurred. The police thought there were three able-bodied men in the house nursing a fourth who had been injured when thrown from the train.

Gill called for reinforcements. He and his men were ready for a fight, as they believed the men inside the house were heavily armed. The old house on Muddy Creek was on the property of a local miller who had not lived in it for some time.

In the meantime, William Coates and William Schmidt had been arrested because they were seen "loafing around" the Big Four yards and at Delhi the day of the robbery. They both had bruises on their faces, and detectives found that most interesting.

Both the raid on the house and the two arrests must have proved to be dead ends, because nothing more was ever written about the incidents.

As the trail grew cold and the newspapers grew interested in other stories, a Big Four detective named Carr stuck with the case. He followed scores of leads and questioned a multitude of people.

Finally, in July 1888, Carr arrested a man named Joe Trenifer for "complicity in the murder of Joe Ketchum." The twenty-five-year-old Trenifer was a member of a gang that included his brother and a man named George Brickly. The trio had a bad reputation, and police felt no crime was beneath them, not even murder. They operated out of a shanty boat on the river in the West End, where Trenifer was known as "Dutch Joe."

The group was well known for terrorizing the outlying districts along the Ohio River. This particular gang had been accused of serial burglaries in the Turkey Bottom area on the same night as a policeman's wedding. Several fellow officers who were friends of the groom deserted their posts that night to attend the reception. Since the neighborhood was left unprotected, Trenifer and his miscreants took advantage. After looting the homes in that area, they worked their way to the center of the city. During the investigation of the housebreakings, detectives tracked the trio to their lair and found burglary tools. Both Trenifers and Brickly were arrested, but the evidence was circumstantial, so all three were let go. Brickly, however, was caught for another job. The charges stuck, and he was relocated to the penitentiary.

As far as Carr was concerned, Trenifer's criminal background was a good enough reason to question him about Joe Ketchum's slaying. Even before the detective gave a reason for the detention, Trenifer said, "I may go to the penitentiary for that Delhi business, but when I get out, I'll kill you." The bravado did not last long, however. As he was questioned in Chief Deitsch's office, he became more and more nervous.

Engineer Jim Boyd was summoned to see if he could identify Trenifer as the man he fought with and threw off the engine. He stood in front of the suspect and said, "Look me right in the eye and say that you are not the man."

At that point, Trenifer was not so nervy. He tried to look at Boyd and tell him he had not been on the train, but his attempt was weak.

"Have you forgot how I took you by the cheek and eye this way?" Boyd asked, grabbing him in a vice-like grip. "Have you forgotten?"

Although Boyd claimed he was the man, Dutch Joe Trenifer was not a boy, nor was he cleanshaven; he had a moustache. About the only similarity between the gang member and the robber Boyd and Fisher tossed from the train was short hair.

Albert Kane Jr., a resident of Delhi, was not sure, but he thought he recognized Trenifer as one of three men who had been hanging around the

Delhi train depot the day before the murder and attempted robbery. His father was more certain. "It is my honest opinion that Trenifer is the man, although I would not swear to it," said the elder Kane. "The man I saw had no moustache—Trenifer has a slight one. Still, he is the man in every other way—form, features and actions."

Lawrence Hazen secured indictments against the James Gang. *Greater Cincinnati Police Historical Society Museum.*

Young Kane added that Dutch Joe was one of three men who "were lurking about our mill for a week before the train robbery." "I would swear to it," he said. "I saw him twice there near father's mill. They slept in the mill at nights. After the robbery, they were never seen again."

The old, one-legged tollgate keeper, Sam Finney, took a look at Trenifer. He thought the man he saw running through the bushes was larger. He added, "For several days previous to the robbery, I had noticed a strange man loitering about. He had a large head and very prominent features. This Trenifer is not the man I saw, but that proves nothing, as I heard three men escaping through the bushes on the night of the robbery." When first asked, he had told police there was only one man running through the brush.

Trenifer averted his eyes in the presence of the witnesses and refused to answer questions.

There does not seem to be any coverage of Trenifer ever being tried for Joe Ketchum's murder.

Chief Larry Hazen had his theory about the crime. "There never was any train robbery intended," he said. "I think, though, that Trenifer was one of the men on the train that night."

Hazen thought that Dutch Joe Trenifer and his gang had been involved in so many ugly dealings in the Cincinnati area that things had gotten too hot for them, so they had moved their shanty boat closer to Delhi, where they would be out of the city and out from under the eyes of the law.

Hazen, who could be blunt and rough in his ways, came out and said that Henry Zimmerman was cowardly. "Zimmerman, the express messenger, ran back through the first and second cars and would likely have run on to the twentieth car if there had been that many on the train."

The way Hazen had it figured, on the night the baggage master was gunned down, Trenifer and his gang boarded the train to ride to the city. "Ketchum had a reputation for bouncing tramps, and he opened the door and smashed one of them over the head and in the fight was killed."

CHAPTER 5
THE DYNAMITE-PROOF SAFE

In the wee hours of July 24, 1895, Express No. 37 was rolling along on the Lake Shore Road about ten miles west of Wauseon, Ohio. The New York & Chicago Express train had originated in Buffalo and was bound for Chicago. It pulled a coach with about two hundred passengers, three sleepers, a baggage car, a smoker and a United States Express money car with a safe carrying what some say was $75,000.

Engineer Mike Tiernan saw nothing out of the ordinary as the train crawled out of a stop at Archbold and gathered speed, heading toward a lonely stretch of road and a place called Reese Siding in Williams County near the Fulton County line. The siding was situated between thick woods on one side and a high bluff on the other. It was a low-speed track that was parallel to the through line and connected at both ends by switches. Its purpose was to allow trains traveling in opposite directions to pass. Isolated from civilization with no telegraph, Reese Siding was the perfect place for a holdup.

Just as the train approached the siding, Tiernan spotted a red light up ahead. That was a signal that the switch had been thrown. The train shot to the sidetrack. As the engineer turned on the air brakes, slackening the speed, a torpedo exploded under the front wheels. At the same time, a volley of bullets shattered the headlamp and ricocheted through the cab.

Two masked men waving guns at Tiernan and the fireman, H. Boardman, leaped into the cab and demanded they raise their hands. The trainmen were ordered down from the engine cab and told to stand in plain view in the ditch. Two more robbers were seen headed back to the express car.

A couple of tramps who had been riding on the front of the baggage car had also seen the red light up ahead and sensed the danger. As soon as the train slackened its speed, the pair jumped off and hid in the ditch. When they heard the explosion and rifle shots, they ran as fast as they could back to Archbold with the intention of getting help.

C.B. Nettleman was the messenger in the United States Express Company car on that run. He recalled for the *New York Times* that the train had been chugging along about forty miles per hour and said there should not have been a stop for another half hour. He thought there was plenty of time for a nap. "I was dozing in my chair near the safe about twelve o'clock last night," he said. "I was surprised and startled when the brakes began to jar on the wheels." When the train came to a stop, Nettleman suspected something was wrong. "I had no sooner come to that conclusion than there was a shock and report under the forward part of my car." The next thing he knew, the window right next to him was blown into "thousands of pieces." He snatched up his shotgun and stood ready at the partially open door.

Through the darkness, he saw the silhouettes of two men, and they were pointing guns right at him. "I dodged back into the car and, raising my gun, let them have it, as I thought, full in the face," he said. "Apparently I did not hit them, and after that they would not stand any monkeying."

"If you put any value in your life, you will put down that gun and let us in," a voice growled. According to another account, the assailants threatened "to blow the whole train over into Indiana."

"Then I gave up," Nettleman said and handed over his shotgun and revolver. "And they came in and went to work." Nettleman told authorities he could not identify any of them because they had tied handkerchiefs over their faces.

The thieves had no problem with the way safe, sometimes called a local safe, which contained small amounts of money being transferred between local stations along the route. They held a gun to the back of Nettleman's head until he handed over the keys for it.

But the big stationary safe in which large sums of money were stowed was a different matter. The messenger had not been entrusted with the combination to it. Even if he had the combination, the safe did not have a dial. It was made that way so it could not be opened between stations. The agent at the terminal point was the only one with the dial that could open that particular safe.

The robbers most likely knew that United States Express Company was a frequent carrier of large amounts of money on Tuesdays and Fridays, so they were not deterred. In anticipation of problems, they had brought dynamite with them. What they did not know was that this stationary safe was dynamite proof.

In frustration, they tried blasting it six different times, according to Nettleman. "Three times they left me in the car while they exploded the dynamite, and three times they took me out," he said. "They kept me 'covered' all the time with their guns." He said he was not frightened until it was all over.

The conductor of the train, William Darling, was sitting in first class when the train suddenly stopped. Experience told him the switch had been turned. He heard a gun volley at the front of the train, a sure signal they were in for trouble. "After sending a brakeman to the rear of the train with a lantern to protect us from anything which might be coming from behind, I went forward into the baggage car and watched what went on from there," recalled Darling. When he stuck his head out, a bullet whizzed past. "I didn't try it again," he told a *New York Times* reporter.

It was dark, but Darling still made out four bandits, and he was able to come up with a sketchy description of one of them. "One of the men was short, heavy-set, with a sandy beard and moustache, about forty years old."

Darling continued, "They stopped the engineer with a red light, and it was afterward found that a pile of ties had been placed across the track."

The explosions woke the passengers and sent the women into a panic. They screamed, and a few even fainted. The men jumped into their clothes and stuffed their watches and money under the mattresses in their berths. One of those passengers was James P. Stark, a clerk in the superintendent's office of the Lake Shore Road. He was sleeping in the smoking car at the time of the robbery. "I was awakened by hearing several shots as the train came to a standstill." The conductor informed him that the train was being held up, but Stark did not go out to investigate, instead choosing to stay put in the smoking car. "Shortly after hearing the shots, I heard four explosions of dynamite," said Stark. "And then all was still, and soon the train pulled out for Stryker, where we arrived at 1:20 a.m."

Although the robbers held the train for forty-five minutes, they made no attempt to rob the passengers. Frustrated at not being able to blow the safe open and swearing a few oaths, the bandits mounted their horses and disappeared into the woods.

When the train pulled into Stryker, Stark went to the express car to survey the damage. He told the *Cleveland Plain Dealer*, "The interior of the car did not appear to be damaged except that the windows had been shot full of

Stryker was the first community in Williams County with railroad facilities. This photograph shows the Lake Shore & Michigan Southern Railroad passenger depot. *Williams County Public Library.*

holes. The only evidence about the through safe was a small dent in the door." His assessment was different than what the superintendent's was when the train reached Chicago.

"The messenger said he saw only four men," Stark said. "When the robbers left the express car, one of them shook hands with the messenger and apologized for putting him to so much trouble."

The tramps who had escaped the robbers made it back to Archbold and reported the holdup. The telegraph operator wired Lake Shore Western Express railroad superintendent Johnson at his home in Toledo. Johnson, in turn, notified both General Manager Canniff and General Superintendent Blodgett, who happened to be in Toledo at the time. The three boarded a special train at three o'clock in the morning and hurried to the scene. They alerted police in all the towns along the way to keep their eyes open for the robbers.

Three hours had elapsed before Wauseon's Sheriff Shaffer and his posse made it to the scene of the crime and scoured the woods. Railroad detectives soon joined them.

The highwaymen had picked the same spot where a gang of horse thieves operated years prior. But that gang had been broken up by vigilantes who

The original Wauseon Depot was built in 1853. Pictured here is the Lake Shore & Michigan Southern Railroad, built in 1895. *Columbus Metropolitan Library.*

hanged some of the thieves. Some of the police thought many of the gang still lived in the area and might be involved.

At first, authorities considered that it could be an inside job—either someone from United States Express Company or their confederates—as the robbers seemed all too familiar with the train. The scoundrels seemed to know the right time to hit the train when there would be no other trains traveling through Reese Siding. They also seemed to know there might be a large amount of money in the money car from New York to Chicago.

Railroad officials refused to give any information on leads their detectives were following, but it was known that several arrests were made the day after the robbery. They had no descriptions to work with, so they simply rounded up tramps or anyone else who looked remotely suspicious. Five men were arrested at Wauseon, and a sixth was taken into custody at Stryker. Lake Shore officials questioned all these men but ultimately released them. They could find no tangible evidence to connect any of these men to the robbery.

The train had continued on and arrived in Chicago around six o'clock that morning, when Messenger Nettleman gave his account to the press. It was noted in the *New York Times* story that as he talked about the robbery, he stopped twice to appeal to Superintendent Wygant of United States Express Company to ensure his approval. He was later closeted with officials and out of the newspaper reporters' reach.

Outlaws often visited saloons. This one was owned by Frank Chappius Sr. Photo taken in 1906. *Williams County Public Library.*

The express car was immediately run onto a sidetrack next to the express company's office. Wygant boarded the car and surveyed the damage from the impact of six dynamite cartridges. He came to a different conclusion on the condition of the inside of the car. Every window was shattered. A board was missing on the side of the car where the safe stood, and the inside wall had been demolished into kindling.

The big safe had a six-inch circular dent where the dial had been blown off. Bits and pieces of it were scattered all over the car. The robbers left a four-inch stick of dynamite behind. The small safe lay open on the floor in the center of the car.

The press had a hard time nailing down the actual loss because all information had to go through Superintendent Wygant, and he was not forthcoming. In fact, the company ordered all the trainmen to avoid the newspapers.

Various rumors had the loss estimated somewhere between $8,000 and $40,000. One of the rumors that surfaced was that the robbers knew $40,000 worth of jewelry had been put on board the train in Cleveland. Another report put the loss at $800 to $1,000. Finally, Superintendent Wygant released a figure of $150. But another express company authority, Frank Benedict, told reporters the loss would be no more than $50. "Anyone can open the little iron safes, but our new dynamite ones are too much for the men with black masks," he said. By the "little iron safes," he meant the way safe. The company was proud of its new dynamite-proof safes. They had been installed in all of the company's express cars after a large loss during a robbery near Kendallville, Indiana, two years prior.

Theodore F. Swayze, private secretary to United States Express Company president Thomas Platt, talked to the *New York Times* on July 26, 1895:

> *The money which was carried off by the robbers was doubtless the contents of the local safe, consisting of small money packages, carried between the different stations on the road. The stationary safe referred to in the dispatch is one of the new kind which have been put into all the money cars of this company recently. The safe weighs three thousand pounds and is fastened to the car by a broad steel band which passes over the top of the safe and is bolted through the floor of the car. It would consume several hours' time to release the fastenings and remove the safe from the car. The safes are of an approved construction, which are guaranteed to be dynamite proof—that is, they cannot be blown open inside of six hours, and no band of robbers can afford to spend so much time over the job.*
>
> *The safes are provided with removable dials, and these dials are in the possession of the agent at the terminal points. The messenger in charge does not know the combination and could not open the safe without the dial. The safes are shipped locked without the dials and can therefore not be opened between stations. The money packages in transit are kept in a smaller, steel safe inside the stationary safe so that we feel sure that every possible precaution is taken to carry money safely. [On] April 4 a train on the Chicago, Rock Island and Texas Railroad was stopped at Dover, Oklahoma, and after the robbers had spent fifty-five minutes in a vain effort to blow open our safe with dynamite, they gave up the job in disgust.*

No amount of prodding by the press would get the express company officials to divulge how much was in the stationary safe. They would only say that the loss would be extremely heavy. The figure that floated around among reporters was $75,000.

The Lake Shore detective who worked on the case believed the robbery was the work of the same gang of farmers who had held up a train at Kessler Siding near Kendallville, Indiana. The methods of operation matched, as did the description of the man who appeared to be their leader. In both robberies, he was referred to as "Jim." The United States Express Company lost $16,000 in that train robbery. A trio of robbers dynamited that safe, and as of the date of the Reese Siding robbery, they were still at large.

In the fall of 1895, Colonel John Byrne, special agent of the United States Express Company, arrested a man named James W. Brown from Michigan for the Indiana robbery. A second man was killed while resisting arrest. The third man was still at large and wanted for murder.

Were these three men responsible for the Reese Siding robbery? It was never recorded. The privately owned United States Express Company went out of business in 1914.

CHAPTER 6
A FUSILLADE OF BULLETS

Harry Errett was just twelve years old when he saw his father murdered in the caboose of a freight train. His father, Jonathan Errett, was a conductor on the Cleveland, Cincinnati, Chicago & St. Louis Railroad, most often called the Big Four. The two were close, and the boy often accompanied his father on runs. On that tragic Wednesday, December 15, 1897, the sixty-year-old railroad man had just received his month's wages at the Linndale yards. That evening at about 7:15, his train, No. 69, pulled out of Linndale traveling toward Berea. Errett and Harry were in the caboose with the rear brakeman, Earl Dalgleish. The conductor and his son sat on the left side of the car while Dalgleish sat working at a desk on the other side.

Moving about twenty miles an hour, the train had reached the west switch a mile past the Big Four depot in Berea. According to young Harry, the front door opened, and two gun-toting thugs wearing red handkerchiefs over the lower parts of their faces burst into the car. He later learned that a third was out on the platform. Harry said of the two that he did see that one was a big man and the other was much smaller. They screamed at everyone to raise their hands. His father refused and instead ordered them to leave the car. The holdup men immediately started firing at the conductor. One news report claimed that Errett pulled his own gun and began shooting.

Young Harry's version differed. "Father sprang at the little man, seizing him by the throat," he said. He told the police and also testified at the coroner's inquest two days after the murder that "the caboose was full of

This majestic old Berea Union Passenger Depot was built of sandstone in 1876. *Berea Historical Society.*

smoke, and I was terribly frightened. I saw father struggling with the little man, who tried to yell, but could not, because father choked him." Both the *Cleveland Plain Dealer* and the *Cleveland Leader* reported that the bandit was beating the father in the head with a coupling pin. Harry said his father pushed the little man through the front door. "I think father threw him off the train," he said.

Brakeman Dalgleish said his back was to the door when the robbers suddenly appeared in the entrance. One of them fired two or three rounds into the ceiling. "I turned and tried to pull my revolver from my pocket," Dalgleish said. "The big man commenced shooting at me, and I jumped for the rear door, getting a bullet in the left shoulder as I went through the door." The bandit ran after him. Dalgleish could not get his gun out of his pocket, so he jumped from the train. He thought eighteen to twenty shots had been fired. The car was so full of smoke that he could not see, but he confirmed there were three bandits all wearing red bandanas over their faces. The one who shot Conductor Errett was about eighteen years old, he thought. It looked to him as though Errett was trying to shield his son.

Once off the train, Dalgleish managed to make his way to the telegraph office and report the shooting. It all happened so fast that he had no chance to help Errett, he said.

Young Harry stated that just as the larger man returned from chasing the brakeman, his father reentered and walked through the car. The boy broke down in tears as he told the police what happened next. "Father walked through the car, passing the car stove on the east side, while the big man passed it going towards the front door on the west side. Father continued walking to the rear end of the car, and as he got to the door, he fell—dead. I ran to him." The boy saw blood flowing from cuts on his father's head. He pulled his father's body completely into the caboose in order to close the door. "I took father's watch and money when I saw that he was dead, and I locked both doors of the caboose." He locked the doors most likely because he was afraid the killers might come back.

The train kept going, and Harry did not know what to do next. He was not able to signal the engineer or head brakeman to stop the train, and he was afraid to try to walk up to the engine because the murderers had disappeared but could still be on board.

When No. 69 reached Columbia Station, three miles away, it slowed down. Harry then grabbed the red lantern, jumped off the train and flagged a pony engine that had been following them.

When the train got to Grafton, the engineer went to the caboose and found the doors locked. Having no idea that anything was wrong, he pried them open and found the dead conductor.

Union Freight Depot was one of the first train stations in Berea. Photo taken in 1910. *Cleveland Press Collection, CSU Michael Schwartz Library.*

Crime was rampant in the northern part of Berea around the passenger and freight depots during this period. With the lack of police protection in the area, it was common for victims to lose their valuables to a thug pointing a gun.

Only a few days before Jonathan Errett's murder, the *Cleveland Plain Dealer* detailed the account of a couple saloon robberies in the neighborhood of the depots. Bullet holes in the bar and walls told the story of the robbery at Foxall's saloon. Four armed men held up two farmers who were playing pool at the saloon on Front Street. When told to put up their hands, the farmers obeyed, but Foxall dove down behind the bar, grabbed his pistol and came up shooting. "They were the nerviest gang of fellows I ever saw," Foxall told the reporter. "I thought I may as well die fighting as run the risk of being robbed and clubbed to death." Even so, the robbers got away with the farmers' valuables. It happened so fast that no one could describe the robbers.

John Wagner was closing his saloon for the night when he heard a knock at the door. He asked who was there. A bullet blasted through the glass in the door. Luckily, he sustained only a flesh wound as the bullet struck his watch, which was in his vest pocket. Wagner recalled three suspicious characters

This saloon, called John's Place, was located south of the city next to the tracks. *Berea Historical Society.*

in his establishment during the day, and he was convinced that they were responsible for the attempted break-in that night.

The article went on to tell about Miss Kate Carney, who lived alone in the northwest part of town. She was awakened by the sounds of someone trying to force open her back door. She quietly fled through the front door to a neighbor's house. A group of local men formed a search party and hunted through the area but came up empty-handed.

A number of murders had been committed on freight trains in that area. Most of the victims were hobos with little or no money who traveled the

Scoundrels often hid among "The Rocks" of Rocky River. The bridge in the background was built about 1909. *Berea Historical Society*.

trains from one city to another looking for work. None of the murders was ever solved.

Criminals also perpetrated a number of assaults on railroad employees, but in each case, the trainmen were able to throw them off the trains. Jonathan Errett was the first railroad employee to lose his life.

Deputy Sheriff J.A. Isling formed a posse to search for the killers. He most likely felt they were looking for the same men who had held up Foxall's saloon, shot at Wagner and even tried to break into Miss Carney's house. Knowing that it was payday, he figured the killers were most likely after Errett's pay.

The posse searched the scene of the holdup. It was a quarter of a mile from the ruins of an old mill near the stone bridge that spanned Rocky River. Its crumbling walls and forgotten machinery had been infested with tramps and thieves for at least twenty years. Large boulders on the riverbanks afforded pockets of hiding places.

Authorities cast a wide net and began detaining anyone within the vicinity of a train or depot who looked mildly suspicious, and a number of men,

This area was known as "The Rocks." The abandoned mill was a perfect hiding place for tramps. *Berea Historical Society.*

some described as tramps, were rounded up. Most promising were three men whom the railroad crew yanked from No. 69's boxcar when the train reached Grafton.

Big Four railroad detective Mellick, who joined the search early on, took the three to Cleveland's Central Police Station. The men were put behind bars but not booked. Although authorities declined to give out their names, it was learned that one of the three was thirty-three-year-old Thomas "Sleepy" Burns, who police believed was a professional tramp associated with the notorious Shore Gang, a group of tramps and highwaymen known for robbery and murder.

Young Harry Errett was taken to the police station to see if he could identify the three men. Burns was a large man with a moustache. Could it have been him? They showed the boy a handkerchief Burns had in his pocket and asked if it looked like the ones the murderers had worn. It looked familiar to the boy, but the detectives said most tramps carried these handkerchiefs.

Burns admitted talking to Harry at the Linndale yard while standing by a warming fire near the track. He asked the boy if he arrived in the pay car. Harry knew it was the pay car, but Burns's rough appearance frightened him, so he said, "No, it was the work car." Burns asked him if he was the conductor's son and if he was on his father's train. The child answered yes to both questions. "I knew at the time that I ought not to have told him," he later said.

By two o'clock the following morning, Akron police had arrested several youths near the train yards but were most interested in two Massillon boys, Otto Bentz and Harry Schaffer, who seemed to fit the description. According to the *Massillon Item*, Harry Errett was taken to Akron to see if he could identify Bentz and Schaffer. He said they were not the shooters. Police checked the boys' stories, and apparently they had been in Akron all morning, so it was impossible for them to have been at the scene of the shooting. Word from Massillon was that the two had good reputations and that one was married. They were released.

Coroner Arbuckle performed an autopsy on Errett and found that he had been shot four times. One bullet entered the right side of his head and fractured his skull. It went through the scalp and exited through the top of his head. Two more pieces of lead were lodged in his intestine, just above the navel. The fourth bullet went into his heart. Burn marks surrounded one of the wounds, indicating that he was shot at very close range.

Jonathan Errett had been a conductor on the Big Four and its predecessors for almost thirty years. He lived with his wife, Mary, and son in Galion, where

Chief of Detectives Jake Lohrer saw more criminal cases through to successful conclusion than anyone else in the department. *Cleveland Police Historical Society Inc.*

he was widely known. The Big Four railroad company assured the public that it would make a determined effort to locate, apprehend and convict the person or persons responsible for his death. The company dispatched a large force of investigators, headed by Detective Mellick, and offered a $500 reward for the capture of the murderers.

On Friday, December 17, the coroner held an inquest into the death at the new morgue on Lake Street in Cleveland. The six men who were implicated in the crime were present, as were Coroner Arbuckle, Detective Mellick and Chief of Detectives Jacob J. "Jake" Lohrer, a Cleveland detective who had worked the evidence in the Blinky Morgan case. Lohrer was also an ex–railroader. Ex–Deputy Coroner O.H.L. Castle conducted the questioning.

When Sleepy Burns was called to the "sweat box" to answer questions, he gave his trade as a metal pattern fitter. He claimed to live at 468 Loth Street in Cincinnati but stated that he had left home after Thanksgiving in hopes of finding work. He vehemently denied having anything to do with the murder, but he did admit to having a conversation with a "little boy" in Linndale just hours before the murder. Burns had asked where the boy lived. Harry told him his father was the conductor of the freight that was getting ready to leave.

Burns said he was most interested in finding out from the boy what the chances were of riding on the train. Harry said his father would not put anyone off as long as they stayed out of sight. Burns denied asking anything in particular about the pay car. Although something was said during the conversation, he could not recall what it was.

Under rigorous questioning, Burns admitted he was often in the company of shady characters and acknowledged that he had been tramping it, using freight trains for transportation. During his examination, he told the authorities that he had landed in Cleveland the previous Tuesday and had gone to look up an old friend, John Zin, a fellow craftsman. He did not find Zin, but he did run into another friend, William Ben Harris. After having a sandwich, Burns found a place to sleep in a stable. The next day, he and Harris set out to find Zin, first at Kelley Manufacturing Company and then at the Walker Manufacturing Company, where they found him. Burns and Harris wound up in Linndale, where they planned to catch a southbound freight.

As No. 69 was pulling out, Burns and Harris jumped up into the boxcar. Burns swore to Castle that he and Harris stayed there until they were arrested in Grafton. He did not see or hear anything out of the ordinary during the trip, although he did look out the door at every stop. At the second stop, he said he saw two men approach the boxcar, stop and then turn and head toward the caboose. It was dark, so he did not get a good look at them.

Castle showed Burns a red handkerchief and asked if it belonged to him. The cloth had been taken from his jail cell in Grafton. He said it looked like his.

Other witnesses that afternoon were William Harris, Frank Winston, Antony Herrick and William Stewart. Herrick and Stewart were two black men arrested by the posse near the old depot.

Harris's story paralleled that of Burns. Under examination, he told of traveling with Burns in hopes of finding work at Galion or maybe Columbus or Cincinnati. He stated that it was he who had asked the child about the pay car. He said as soon as he got on the train, he fell asleep and knew nothing about the murder until two officers pulled him out of the car at Grafton. He denied having a red bandana, but he saw the officers take one from Burns.

Antony Herrick also denied any knowledge of the murder. He had been in the workhouse until the day of the murder, working off a fine of $4.50 for intoxication. After he was released, he tried to gain employment through the YMCA, but because he was not a member, it would not help him. He tried getting employment at the breweries on the west side of Cleveland but had no luck there. Eventually, he found his way to Linndale and Conductor Errett's freight train. He claimed that he did not see Burns or Harris during the trip and found out about the murder only when he was arrested.

One of the men dragged off the train at Grafton was Frank Winston of Windsor, North Carolina. When his turn in the "sweat box" came, he said he had been working for a doctor in Cumberland, Maryland. When that job was finished, he went on to Pittsburgh, Youngstown and, finally, Cleveland looking for work. He started out for Columbus but got on the wrong train, so he doubled back and wound up in Linndale, where he caught the train to Grafton.

William Stewart gave his home as Bellefontaine, Ohio. He, too, was in search of a job, and he walked to Linndale from Cleveland and boarded the train on the night of the murder. According to the *Plain Dealer*, he told a "very straight story."

Lake Shore Detective Bridgestone was a spectator at the inquest. He came to see Thomas Burns testify because he was convinced that Burns was also known as "Black" Murphy, a most dangerous road agent. Bridgestone said Black Murphy often traveled with "White" Murphy, who was sometimes known as Murphy No. 2. Bridgestone told Cleveland police how Black Murphy was captured near Sandusky after a desperate fight but escaped custody. "He is a dangerous man," Bridgestone told the other lawmen. "He's a member of the Shore Gang."

On Monday, young Harry Errett took the stand and in a straightforward but graphic manner told the story of his father's murder. After he was finished, each of the suspects was brought before him for identification. Each was dressed in the "rigging" that the murderers were supposed to have worn. Harry carefully looked each man over and each time declared, "He is not the man."

Brakeman Earl Dalgleish gave his version of the murder and also viewed the suspects. He agreed with Harry that none of them had killed Conductor Errett.

After the inquest, all the men were let go. None of them could definitely be tied to the murder.

By Christmas, it seemed like the case had gone cold. Cleveland Police Chief George Corner said he could not justify detectives spending any more time on a case that was outside their jurisdiction. He said that Cleveland detectives were paid by Cleveland to do city work, and Errett's murder was beyond the four-mile limit.

Detective Mellick refused to give up on the case and went back to square one in Berea to try to gather more evidence. He worked night and day in hopes of tracking down the killers.

Cleveland Police Chief George E. Corner (1896–1903) brought down the Foster Gang as a young patrolman. *Cleveland Police Historical Society Inc.*

He caught a break a few days after the murder when he found a piece of cloth on the Lake Shore tracks. It matched up with a torn curtain in the caboose where Errett was killed. There were brown stains on it. After it was examined under a microscope, it was determined the stains were blood. Mellick theorized that it had been torn from the curtain to wrap a wound.

Through sheer perseverance, Mellick found what he thought was the culprits' escape route. They had boarded a Detroit Street car and ridden to the Square in Cleveland. There, they had boarded a car bound for Bedford. At Bedford, they had hopped a freight car bound for DeForest Junction, a small town in Trumbull County on the B&O. There was a camp near the railroad there where a gang of tramps stayed.

Toward the end of December, Mellick arrested two men who seemed to know too much about the murder to not be involved. He found them near DeForest Junction, according to the *Akron Beacon Journal*. The *Plain Dealer* accounts claimed the men delivered the names of the shooters to Mellick and that they were members of a notorious Pittsburgh gang of thieves and tramps. Word had it that they could be found at the camp near DeForest, where traveling gangs were accustomed to congregating.

Mellick knew there could be at least thirty to forty well-armed tramps at the DeForest site. He wanted to arrest all of them, but he knew he needed help. Whether he teamed up with Cleveland police or other railroad detectives, Mellick must have gotten the help he needed. He went out to raid the camp the next night, but he was hugely disappointed. The camp was deserted; all that was left was one smoldering fire. Mellick was certain that someone had given warning to the inhabitants.

After the first of the year, Pennsylvania Railroad Police Captain G.S. Ward and Detective C.E. Stone arrested five men in Hudson in connection with a train robbery in Orville. Shortly after taking them into custody, the officers began looking at them for the Errett murder. It seems that one of them made a remark that if the gang was arrested and taken to Cleveland, their "goose would be cooked." Ward and Stone took this to mean they knew something about the Big Four conductor's murder.

The men gave their names, ages and home cities: Charles Martin, twenty-two, Detroit; Arthur A. Marshall, thirty-nine, Chicago; Frank Kennedy, twenty-six, Sandusky; Frank Whitman, twenty-eight, Detroit; and Robert Walker, thirty-six, Cleveland.

The Berea Union Depot closed in 1958. Restored in 1980, it is now a popular restaurant and tavern. *Berea Historical Society.*

Martin and Marshall were on their way to the coast to obtain jobs on board a ship. Kennedy had been in the hospital. He and Whitman tramped together to Canton. Walker was already known to police for having been a guest in the workhouse due to several minor offenses.

Martin and Marshall were held as witnesses because they gave a "tip" against the other three. At least three other railroad detectives, including Mellick, were sure Kennedy, Whitman and Walker were members of the Shore Gang, which was credited with Conductor Errett's murder. A few days later, four of those men were released. The fifth man, Robert Walker, was taken back to Youngstown, where he was wanted for breaking into a train car.

Nearly a year later, authorities still had not caught the killers. Law enforcement agencies in the area dutifully followed leads and questioned numerous suspects, but they always came up empty-handed. Each time they dragged tramps or other suspicious characters into Cleveland for questioning, they brought Harry Errett in to identify them. Each time, Harry could not. At one point, the village of Berea had spent so much money on the case that it almost went bankrupt. In the end, all the detectives agreed that every interview, every clue, led them back to the Shore Gang.

CHAPTER 7

MESSENGER THREATENED, BOUND HAND AND FOOT

Two of the boldest devils ever to don a mask and grasp a pistol" held up a Cincinnati, Sandusky & Cleveland (CS&C) train and came close to killing its messenger, according to a special dispatch to the *Cleveland Leader*. The robbery happened in the early morning hours of Thursday, October 2, 1890, between Urbana and West Liberty.

There were many conflicting accounts of this robbery given by the trainmen themselves and in newspapers of the time. However, all the records agreed that the northbound CS&C No. 2 pulled out of Urbana right on time at 3:20 a.m. and that Arch L. Scudder was the Adams Express messenger on that train. Scudder was fifty years old and was called an "old-time express man." He had been on the line since Adams Express took charge of the road about three years before. Prior to that, he was an Adams messenger on the trains running along the Ohio River and had lived in Cincinnati for some years.

Scudder told a reporter at the *Champaign Democrat* a few days after the crime that he was just settling down to business in the express car after leaving Urbana. "I was sitting with my back to the door," he said. "The door was locked but did not have the bar up." All seemed to be going well until two men forced open the door of the express car and confronted him with guns. One of the men stared out at Scudder from behind a green mask, while his partner hid his identity with a dirty white one. "They came up to me, each one with a revolver in his hand and pointing it at me, demanding my keys, telling me to hold up my hands," he told the reporter excitedly.

The Pennsylvania Station and No. 7 at Urbana. *Champaign County Public Library*.

It took Scudder a split second to size them up. One weighed about 180 pounds, he thought, and the other about 160. He knew they meant business. His own gun, a .22-caliber pistol, was out of reach across the coach. If he tried to grab it, he surely would be dead before he could lay a hand on it. The odds were against him, so he decided not to offer any resistance. He held up his hands.

One of them produced a clothesline from under his overcoat and bound the messenger's hands and feet. "They first told me to lay down. I told them I could not do it, tied as I was," Scudder said. "They picked me up and threw me down, then took the keys out of my pocket." They also relieved him of his watch and $1.50.

"They snapped a pistol at me and made me give up the keys," recalled Scudder. During the process, one of the robbers dropped the safe key "and could not unlock it for some time." This unnerved the villainous pair so much that one of the masked scoundrels held the muzzle of his gun to Scudder's temple and threatened to kill him. "They came back to me and told me if I did not want to die to give up the key." He told them he did not have it, that it was on the floor somewhere. "They had a pistol to my head and again demanded the key."

The robber who was covering Scudder cocked his gun and pulled the trigger. Luckily, the cartridge failed to explode.

"Don't kill him, Jack," his pal interceded, calling him by name. In some reports, the name was Jake.

West Liberty Depot and American and National Express companies. *Logan County Historical Society and Museum.*

Just then, one of them spotted the key on the floor. He scooped it up and jammed it into the safe's lock while the other kept the gun leveled at Scudder's head.

"They got about $400 out of the safe," Scudder said. "And they got an envelope with between $50 or $60 belonging to me." (Scudder had been paid his salary the previous evening.)

"When they threw me down," Scudder added, "they threw me on my stomach and hurt me. This was about the roughest treatment I got from them. After getting the money, they stood in the car until West Liberty, when they went out. One had on an overcoat, the other a short sack coat. One had a Derby hat, the other a soft one."

The train stopped at West Liberty, but there was no express to take on board and no goods to offload, so no one at the depot was aware of the robbery. Five hundred yards below the depot, the train made a second stop at a railroad crossing. At this point, the robbers jumped off the train. William Milliner of Urbana witnessed the two dive under a freight train and disappear through the alley of the lower quarter of town. One of them dropped his mask, so Milliner got a fairly good look at him. He described him as "a heavy-set man, weighing about 190 pounds, and smooth faced. The other was smaller and would not weigh over 160 pounds."

For some reason, the nefarious pair rounded back to the train and climbed aboard the front end of the baggage car. The trainmen found the two men hiding there but were pushed back at gunpoint and held at bay until the train reached Bellefontaine, at which point the bandits jumped off CS&C No. 2 and hopped a southbound freight. Police later recovered some items of clothing, which they held for evidence.

There are two different accounts as to how Scudder was freed. In one, he told the *Champaign Democrat* that a man waiting at the West Liberty depot came to the door of the express car: "While here, William Fishbaugh came to the door and knocked, and asked if I had a corpse, which it appears he was expecting. I told him I had not and also told him I had been robbed, and to inform the conductor, Mr. Bosworth, which he did."

Apparently, as the train was leaving West Liberty, the baggage master and brakeman tried to come into the car but were driven back by the robbers and their pistols. The train continued on to Bellefontaine with the two desperados on board.

"I managed to get both arms out from the ropes, and I was waiting for an opportunity to use my revolver when we slowed up at the Bee Line crossing in Bellefontaine," Scudder recalled. "I heard them jump and fired one shot at them as they did so."

In another newspaper report, it was a seventeen-year-old newsboy named Orrie Knight at Bellefontaine who went to the car for papers and heard Scudder crying out for help. He found the messenger lying on his stomach with ropes binding him from head to toe. Young Knight said that although some of the rope had been wound around Scudder's neck and was nearly choking him, "the tying was a bungling job."

The stop was a short one at Bellefontaine. After Scudder was freed, he was too excited to give any information on the affair. There are differing accounts as to when and where the authorities were alerted. At any rate, the culprits had plenty of time to make their getaway. Both the crew and the passengers on the train knew what happened, but no one made any effort to chase after the pair. When No. 2 pulled out for Sandusky fifteen minutes later, Scudder was still in the express car.

At eight o'clock the following morning, the forty-year-old first-term Sheriff Wallace W. Roach and Deputy J.C. Sullivan got into a gun battle with three men who jumped from a train just north of Bellefontaine. They thought they had the robbers cornered. When the gun smoke cleared, the sheriff and his deputy prevailed against two of the men. There were no casualties, but a third man escaped after a "hard run," police said. The two were carted off to jail and questioned, but neither was talking. They even refused to give their names or addresses.

It was noted that the prisoners somewhat fit the descriptions of the robbers of the CS&C No. 2 train. Neither of the men had any facial hair. One was five-foot-ten and weighed about 170 pounds. His partner was five-foot-eight and weighed about 150 pounds.

Finally, one of the suspects asked, "Did the big fellow get away?" He claimed the third man had done all the shooting. They were still mum on their names and addresses, but police learned that the day before the robbery, the prisoners had hopped a Big Four train bound for De Graff, southwest of Bellefontaine, and returned on the fast train. When police spotted them, they were on the platform of the baggage car. The culprits bolted after laying eyes on the law. Then the shooting began.

Sheriff Roach figured the third man who got away probably had the swag. The police also thought he may have stood guard during the robbery. Cincinnati Police Chief Detective Lawrence Hazen, who had a wide background in detective work as an express detective and as the owner of his own agency, was called in to help. His son, William, who went on to become the head of the Secret Service, was also pressed into service. They joined Roach and Sullivan on a special engine to go after the third suspect.

It was reported that five Pinkerton agents also landed on the case. This may or may not have been true. Pinkerton had around thirty thousand reserves by the early 1890s, and the State of Ohio outlawed the agency because it feared the possibility of a private army or militia. At any rate, it appeared that Wallace and Hazen, both very popular and smart, were more than able to handle the case. They chased their man twenty-two miles north to Kenton and captured him that evening. After questioning him, they were satisfied that he was not one of the train robbers, but they took him into custody as a valuable witness against the other two. He did confess to being with them when they tried to burglarize a house in Urbana hours before the holdup.

Estimates of how much money was taken ranged anywhere from $1,000 down to $300. One report came out that more than $40,000 was taken, but Scudder put the loss at around $400, although he may not have known what all was in the eleven packages the scoundrels shoved in their pockets. Some speculated there could have been bank funds in the packages, or jewelry—maybe diamonds—worth quite a bit.

Had the villains attacked the previous morning's train, they would have made away with a $38,900 payroll made up of salaries of all the employees along the line. Perhaps they miscalculated.

A few weeks later, Sheriff Roach and Deputy Sullivan arrested a twenty-year-old man at the Bellefontaine depot. Strangely, he was carrying green goggles and a false moustache in his valise. Without the moustache, his face was smooth. He was five-foot-eight inches tall and weighed about 160 pounds, fitting the description of one of the train robbers. When police searched him, they found a train ticket to Indianapolis, $371.23 in cash, six diamonds and a .44-caliber revolver. The paper money was wet. Two of the diamonds had been pried from their settings in earrings. He also had in his possession two pawn tickets worth $18 from a Kansas City pawnshop.

Roach learned that his suspect had come in to Bellefontaine on a Big Four train from the west and registered as J.E. Williams at the Commercial Hotel. He was later identified as J. Frank Smith, a telegraph operator, recently from Urbana. Whether his first name was Jack or Jake was not reported.

On the morning before he was arrested, Smith hired a livery rig and drove to a farmhouse owned by John McColloch. The house was in a lonely spot near the Deep Cut, three and a half miles out from the city. The farmer grew suspicious when Smith came back a second time and asked for directions to West Liberty. The young stranger said he wanted to go there, but when he drove off, he went in the opposite direction.

A young neighbor named Jewell, who lived on the Ludlow road, was also suspicious after finding some watchcases and express envelopes in his barn. He drove into town to show them to the police.

This depot was built about 1898 and caught fire in 1946. It housed a restaurant in the back. *Logan County Historical Society and Museum.*

By the time Roach and Sullivan got out to the Deep Cut area, the suspect was gone, but they followed his tracks to a nearby swamp, where it looked like someone had been digging. Police came back into town and nabbed him at the depot just as he was getting on a westbound train.

Under questioning, Smith said he had been working as a telegrapher on the Santa Fe route and that he was on his way back there. He explained the diamonds by saying he was peddling them. He had no answer as to why the money was soggy, but police knew it had been buried in the swamp. He told Sheriff Roach he was out in the country because he was looking for an old friend from Urbana. He told the livery that he was going to Rushsylvania, a town northeast of Bellefontaine, to look up a relative named Neer.

Further investigation turned up the name of O.S. Robinson, who had been an agent of the CS&C at Urbana. He was Smith's brother-in-law.

A short time after the arrest, Jewell, who had originally called attention to Smith, was working in his barn. He found four more watchcases with the workings removed. One was a key winder, and three had stems. All were German made. He also found an express package and papers belonging to Arch L. Scudder. The package contained $120 and was addressed to a Sandusky man. There was a receipt for $400 from R.C. Carter, local secretary, Division No. 41, Express Aid Society, for contribution No. 259 dated September 15, 1890. It bore Scudder's name. An envelope addressed to A.L. Scudder was also among the findings. It probably held his salary. The last thing found was a beat-up photograph of three women or a family. It was in such poor condition that the inscription on it was unreadable.

Smith was held in the Bellefontaine jail until Detective Will Hazen, Larry Hazen's son, took him to Urbana and brought him before Justice Galligher. Smith took the advice of his attorney, J.M. Lewis, and waived a preliminary examination. He was charged with robbing the CS&C No. 2 on the morning of October 2, 1890, bound over to the grand jury and placed under $2,000 bond. Not able to make the bond, he was turned over to the sheriff and locked up.

Chief Lawrence Hazen did more than hunt criminals. In 1860, HRH Albert Edward, Prince of Wales and the future king of Great Britain, visited the United States and Canada. It was Hazen's job to escort the eighteen-year-old, his chaperone, the Duke of Newcastle and the rest of the royal party on their sightseeing trip. One night while in St Louis, Hazen and the prince slipped away from the watchful eye of the duke and the others to tour the "night life" of the city.

CHAPTER 8
HE DID IT FOR LOVE

When the eastbound Panhandle No. 8 passenger train pulled into Union Station in Columbus at 11:40 p.m., August 10, 1900, the Adams Express agent approached the express car. He opened its door and was faced with a gruesome scene.

Charles Lane, the twenty-eight-year-old messenger, was lying in the forward part of the car in a pool of blood, his body riddled with bullets. Before touching anything, the agent summoned Columbus city and Adams Express detectives.

It looked to the express company's investigator, Robert Mulligan, and Coroner J.W. Birmingham as if Lane had been taken by surprise. He had three holes in his back. Some of the slugs were visible through the skin on his chest. Another bullet was lodged in his side, and there were four pieces of lead in his right leg. Two more .38-caliber bullets rolled around on the floor. A closer examination revealed he had also sustained a heavy blow to the head. His body was cold to the touch, and the blood had started to clot.

One of the two safes was wide open and had been cleaned out. The keys hung in the lock, so investigators thought the murderer or murderers might have run out of time.

Lane's gun was sitting on top of the safe. Two or three cartridges had been fired, leading city police to believe he had tried to defend himself.

Mulligan had a hunch that only one man did the job and that Lane never got a chance to get a shot off. He thought the murderer shot Lane

Columbus Union Station was built in 1897 to alleviate traffic problems on North High Street. *Columbus Metropolitan Library.*

in the leg to disable him. Once Lane was crippled, the shooter got the key and opened the safe.

The robber must have found Lane's gun inside the safe and decided to use it to finish off the agent. Mulligan believed that Lane knew the robber and that was why he was killed.

The evidence in the car suggested that Lane had been murdered close to Columbus. It was obvious that he had washed up, shucked off his overhauls and donned his street clothes in preparation to go home. His book had been posted and ready to turn over to the messenger who would succeed him on the run east from Columbus. Packages were neatly stacked, and his portfolio was in the safe. His penknife was lying open next to his body, so it looked as though he had used it to cut string on some of the packages.

Conductor Jerry Taylor told police he saw and talked with Lane at Urbana. According to another member of the train crew, Lane stuck his head out of the side door of his car at Milford Center, so he was still alive at that point.

John Fletcher, the baggage master, was riding in the car immediately behind the express car and had gone to Lane's car during the earlier part of the evening, where he found the door open because of the heat and humidity. "After we left Urbana, everything went well until we reached Capell, where we made a stop," Fletcher recalled. "I heard talking there. The speakers first appeared to be coming along beside the train, there being two or three of them. One man stepped on a piece of rotten wood, which attracted my attention just before the train got under way. We stopped at Plain City and Milford, and I heard no unusual sounds. After we left Plain City, I thought I would wash up and tried the door of the express car, but found that it would only move about an inch. I concluded that Lane had freight against it." Fletcher thought the time was about 11:00 p.m.

It made police wonder whether the robber or robbers could have been in the car at that time. "We stopped at Marble Cliff, and there I saw two men running toward the train. One was an old man, and the other a young fellow. Both were dressed in dark clothes," Fletcher added.

J.W. Beckett, the night ticket agent, thought the configuration of the train might have had some bearing on why the murder was not immediately discovered. The express car was between two mail cars. The first mail car was right behind the engine. Next came the express car and then the other mail car. Mail cars had blind baggage ends so that no one could pass through from one coach to another. This, along with the engine noise, may have deadened the sounds of gunfire.

Pennsylvania Railroad and Adams Express officials joined Columbus police in the search, as did police departments for fifty miles around Columbus. They chased leads and questioned anyone who looked mildly suspicious. They learned of a man who got on the train and paid his fare but was not seen getting off, unless he jumped off the train right outside the depot.

No. 8's fireman saw three men board the train at Milford. He could not say where on the train they went, but he knew they did not present themselves to the conductor.

Two tramps were arrested in Plain City because they could not give a satisfactory accounting for their time. Police searched for a third man who stopped the train to board at Marble Cliff, four miles west of Columbus, which might have given the robbers the chance to escape. Later that day, the tramps were let go, but not before giving police the description of yet another man who might have been implicated in the crime.

Above: This Plain City scene shows the view looking west down the tracks. The depot is at the right. *Plain City Historical Society*.

Left: Acting Chief of Detectives Patrick Kelly became the assistant superintendent of Columbus Police in 1895. *Columbus Metropolitan Library*.

A local farmer presented himself at police headquarters with a story of three men who had menaced him when he caught a ride on Pennsylvania train No. 8 from Milford Center to Marble Cliff.

Police followed any lead that sounded the least bit promising, but none panned out.

A special detail of Columbus detectives Thomas E. Foster, James A. Dundon and Thomas F. O'Neill was sent back over the Panhandle route to scour the countryside for evidence. Their instructions were to report back to Patrick Kelly, who acted as the chief of detectives at the time.

There are two stories regarding who finally cracked the case. While Foster takes credit in his biography, *Trails in Shadowland: A Detective's Wild Ride*, written by Alonzo B. Shaw, the newspapers of the day most often cited O'Neill and Dundon, who later became Columbus's first official chief of detectives. Foster's name is mentioned a few times in the papers as he retraced the route back to Plain City.

At daybreak on Saturday, the detectives found a hotel in Plain City and asked its proprietor, Barney Smiley, if any strangers had registered the night before. Smiley did not recall seeing anyone around the hotel. Later in the day, the investigators went back to the hotel. This time, Smiley did remember a man who came in very late and stayed the night but had forgotten to register. Smiley said he was half asleep at the time, so he did not get a good description. He showed the detectives the room where the man had slept, and they gave it a thorough search. O'Neill and Dundon's big break came when they found a .38-caliber revolver between the mattress and bedspring. Waybills and checks had also been left behind, probably in haste.

At the station, they heard the stranger had expressed a package before leaving on the train to Columbus that same morning. They immediately

Barney Smiley's Hotel Smith (far left) is likely where Ferrell stayed in Plain City the night of the murder. *Plain City Historical Society*.

called Columbus Police Inspector Thomas G. Baron and had him intercept it. He confiscated the package and opened it. Inside were Adams Express bags containing checks, money orders and waybills.

When the detectives returned to Columbus, they met with Chief Detective Kelly and began putting the pieces together. Given the evidence, the only thing that made sense was that Lane knew his killer. The evidence pointed toward the possibility that the murderer might be an ex-employee of the Adams Express Company. Their next move was to pay a visit to the express office to find out if any employees had been fired recently. The company's files revealed that an agent named Ross Ferrill had been discharged three months prior, let go after three complaints had been waged against him for broken packages. The file contained a detailed description of him that fit the sketchy one given by Smiley, the hotel keeper in Plain City.

The detectives learned that the suspect's name was actually Rosslyn Ferrell and that he had been out of town Friday night and returned Saturday morning. He also matched the description of the man who sent the express package from Plain City.

Ferrell lived on West First Avenue in a boardinghouse owned by Mr. and Mrs. J.L. Montfort, but he was not home when O'Neill and Dundon went there. They searched his room and found a suit with twenty-seven dollars in the pocket and a watchcase. Neighbors said he was most likely at his sweetheart's house. Her name was Miss Lillian Costlow, and she lived on Twenty-first Street on the east side of the city.

Whether to head off any violent attempts at escape or to preserve the young lady's dignity, O'Neill and Dundon concocted a story to tell Ferrell once they were face to face with him. They knocked on the door of the Costlow house and asked to see Ferrell. They

William Pitt Tyler was the marshal in Deadwood, South Dakota, before serving as Columbus police chief. *Columbus Metropolitan Library*.

were invited into the sitting room, where they found an attractive young man with dark hair talking with his lady. Their presence seemed to annoy him. When the six-foot-tall and well-built man rose from his chair, the detectives decided the description from the express company was exactly right. The officers told him he was suspected of a burglary and asked him to go with them to headquarters to talk with the superintendent of police, William Pitt Tyler.

Ferrell was probably relieved. "I guess there must be some mistake," the twenty-two-year-old said confidently. He excused himself and accompanied the detectives.

On the way to the police headquarters, O'Neill and Dundon told Ferrell they actually wanted to talk to him about Lane's murder. They told him what they already knew and showed him the watch.

"I never saw that watchcase," he said.

"Well, we found it in your clothes at your boarding house. And what about the $27?"

The stress was evident on his face and posture. "I saved it," he answered.

When the detectives showed him the gun they found in the hotel room, he began to crack. Within the hour, he admitted to the cold-blooded murder and told police an incoherent story of what happened, breaking down several times as he told it. "I needed money," he said. "I was discharged from the Adams Express Company two months ago, and I've been unable to secure employment since then. I needed money badly. Lillian and I are to be married this coming Thursday, and I have to have money for the marriage."

Ferrell knew Panhandle No. 8 ran between St. Louis and Columbus and that the way safe always carried a considerable amount of money, so he made his plans. First, he got his hands on a Smith & Wesson, six-shot, .38-caliber revolver, and on Friday morning, he rode the westbound train to Urbana, where he then waited for No. 8. When the train rolled in, Ferrell went to Lane and asked to ride to Columbus in the express car with him, explaining that he did not have enough money for a ticket.

During the first part of the ride, the two chatted amicably. At one point, Lane sat down in a chair at the end of the car with his back slightly turned. Ferrell had finally worked up his nerve. He drew his revolver and pumped three shots into Lane's back and kept shooting until his gun was empty.

Ferrell looked around the car and saw Lane's revolver. He picked it up, shot Lane two or three more times and then snatched the keys for the way safe from the dead man's pocket. As he opened the safe, he laid Lane's gun on the shelf within easy reach in case he was detected and needed to defend himself. He grabbed up all the money packages, money orders and waybills from the safe

and crammed them into a satchel he had brought with him. When the train slowed down at Plain City, he quietly slipped off.

After walking around for a while to gain his composure, he found a hotel, took a room and retired for the night. The innkeeper was half asleep and did not notice that he had not registered. In his room, he went through the package and separated out the cash. He had to get rid of the waybills, money orders and, of course, his gun. The gun was simple; he stuffed it between the mattress and springs on the bed. Finally, he hit on the idea of packaging up all the waybills and money orders and expressing them to a fictitious name in a distant city, knowing the package would be unclaimed and unopened there for some time. He then lay down and tried to sleep.

Top: Adams Express messenger Charles Lane was murdered aboard Pennsylvania express train No. 8. *Illustration by Justin Campbell.*

Left: Rosslyn H. Ferrell murdered Charles Lane to get money for his impending marriage. *Illustration by Justin Campbell.*

The Plain City Depot. *Plain City Public Library.*

Ferrell rose early the next morning and went down to the station to express the package to a fictitious C.W. Caylor in Lockport, New York. He bought a ticket and boarded the train for Columbus at 6:30 a.m. When he got back to Columbus, he went to his boardinghouse to change his clothes. Everywhere he turned, people were talking about the murder and robbery. It upset him, but he kept up the façade. During the day, he paid bills with the money he had stolen and bought himself a new suit. That evening, he went to see Lillian and arranged to see her again the next afternoon when he was arrested.

After hearing Ferrell's story, Superintendent Tyler asked him to commit his confession to paper. It appeared in the August 13, 1900 *Plain Dealer*:

> *My name is Charles R.H. Ferrell, and my parents live in Steubenville, Ohio. I formerly worked for the Adams Express Company but was discharged two months ago. I was to be married to Miss Lillian Costlow next Thursday, and I needed money. This is what caused me to do as I have done. I looked for work and did not find it, and the thought of being idle and without money made me reckless. On Friday I thought I might get some money in the way I did get it, and I immediately began to lay my plans.*
>
> *I went to Urbana Friday afternoon about four o'clock with the messenger on No. 33 and left the train at Urbana. I knew Mr. Lane slightly, having*

met him several times when he first came to Columbus. He had not been over long. When No. 8 came into Urbana, I boarded the express car, and Mr. Lane, knowing me and knowing that I had been a messenger, let me in the car. I cannot tell how long I was in the car nor where I got off, and I have but little recollection of what occurred. I know that when I got ready to go to work, Mr. Lane was standing with his back to me. I fired on him, and he started to run for the door. He did not make a sound until he got to the door. When he got there, he cried out. I shot him several times, emptying my gun. I then took the money and goods from the safe and then shot Lane again with his own revolver. I do not know how many times I shot him with his own revolver. I left the car at the next stop. I did not know the name of the town, and a man told me where I could find a hotel. I went to the room and fixed the envelopes and other evidence of the robbery and made them up in a package to get rid of them and shipped them to Lockport, New York, in the name of C.W. Caylor by way of Cleveland. After getting the money, I did not count it, and I do not yet know how much there was of it. I could not sleep, but lay tossing on the bed. I went to the train next morning after placing the package in the express office and came to the city.

Thomas George Baron retrieved the Adams Express money from Ferrell's sweetheart. *Columbus Metropolitan Library.*

Ferrell signed the confession and was led away to a cell, where he collapsed. The guards were ordered to watch him to "make sure he did not do any harm to himself." That evening, Ferrell calmed down considerably, ate a hearty supper and smoked a cigar.

By going back over Ferrell's story, police determined the robbery and murder were committed in Union County, and that court would have jurisdiction. The prisoner would be held at Marysville until his court date.

Ferrell had given Lillian the rest of the money for safekeeping, telling her it was money he had saved from work. The job of recovering that money from Lillian fell to Columbus Police Inspector Thomas G. Baron. It was a task he did not relish.

Lillian was the daughter of Julia and Patrick Costlow, an engineer on the Pittsburgh Railroad. When a member of the Columbus police came calling a second time and explained the circumstances, the bride-to-be broke down. Neither she nor her parents had any indication that Ferrell was anything but a model young man. He had lavished attention on Lillian and claimed, "I do not use tobacco, read dime novels nor swear." Baron recovered just over $1,000 from the young woman. Police thought that was the total Ferrell had stolen, except for about $150 he used to pay bills and buy a suit. The issue of the watchcase never came up again.

Grant Curtis, division superintendent of Adams Express, said about $1,200 was stolen, and most of that had been recovered. Money orders that Ferrell had stowed away in a vault at his boardinghouse had also been returned.

Later that month, Curtis drafted a list of messengers who would be discharged for violating company rules by allowing Ferrell and other discharged employees to ride in express cars. The first to lose his job was a messenger who had allowed Ferrell to ride in his car. The list, which was not made public, caused a good deal of anxiety among the messengers, as it was a rule that was commonly broken.

Police continued questioning Ferrell. Each time he told his story, more revolting details came out. He gave several different versions of how he shot Lane. In his initial version, Lane

Grant Curtis, division superintendent of Adams Express, discharged employees who let previous messengers ride in express cars. *Columbus Metropolitan Library.*

95

was sitting in a chair. In another version, Lane was standing by the door. In still another, Lane was tying his shoelace.

Ferrell was always clear that he needed money. He did not even have streetcar fare. He owed for his lodging, his board, his laundry and the medicine he had used. He was intent on getting the money he thought he needed. He was wildly in love with Lillian Costlow, but without money, he was afraid their pending marriage would be postponed, and he could not have that happen.

Ferrell was a contradiction of emotions. He would suffer from nervous exhaustion and near collapse, and then a few hours later, he would regain his strength and confidence and be perfectly calm. At times, he would talk freely as if nothing was bothering him. But other times, he was obviously in the depths of despair and would profess to gladly give his life if it were "all to be done over."

"The Adams Express could place in my charge all its money," he cried at one point, "and I would not touch a cent. One minute after I fired those shots, I knew the horror of it, and I would have given my life and all to have had that car as it was before I shot." He was in such a state of despair at one point that authorities called a doctor to examine him. The doctor thought he was "scamming" them, but Superintendent Tyler wanted him watched for fear he would attempt suicide.

Early one morning, Dr. Carl Louis Perin came calling at the jail, according to a *Plain Dealer* account. He was a traveling practitioner of palmistry. It was highly irregular, but someone outside the police department had requested this "exam." Curiously, Mayor Samuel J. Swartz was one of those who watched as Perin read Ferrell's palms. The doctor claimed Ferrell was born a murderer but that his lifeline was long, unbroken and sharply defined. "How could that be?" someone asked. "He's most likely going to die in the electric chair."

"Lines only indicate traits of strength or weakness, and the man himself could destroy those chances," Perin answered.

Tobias Ferrell heard of his son's arrest through a rumor and called the Columbus police from Steubenville to find out. Authorities told him it was true: his son, Rosslyn H. Ferrell, was accused of murder, and he had confessed. The elder Ferrell, who was a bridge carpenter and well-respected citizen, made the trip to Columbus. He was visibly shaken when he saw his son behind bars, but he did not break down. In a strong, calm voice, he said, "The only thing left for you to do is to look to the good of your soul. There is nothing else in all the world for you now. I trained you in honesty and an upright life, and it has come to this."

The grief-stricken father then went to visit the Costlows and told Lillian that his wife was terribly distressed and would never have believed her son was capable of such an act if he had not confessed. He was afraid his wife would never recover from the blow.

Lillian Costlow wanted to see Ferrell. She had wept uncontrollably in the previous days, argued with her father and discussed it with her friends, but she had made up her mind. She implored her father to accompany her to the jail, and he had finally given in. To avoid the crowds and newspapers, she visited his cell at two o'clock in the morning. It was said that Ferrell could barely rise up from his cot and that she had to help him. The two spoke quietly. As she was leaving, they kissed and he asked her to write to him. Her only answer was tears, and the guard led her away.

Her visit must have gone a long way in giving Ferrell peace, because he slept until he was awakened at 5:30 a.m. to take the train to Marysville for his preliminary hearing. He was in a good frame of mind until it was time to leave, and then he collapsed. Detectives Dundon and O'Neill carried him to the train with Tyler helping. Inspector Baron, Chief Detective Kelly, Detective Foster and Superintendent Curtis accompanied them on the trip. As soon as the train pulled out, his nervousness was gone, and he began talking and smoking cigars.

The preliminary hearing took place at 8:00 a.m. before Mayor Charles Hamilton. Curiosity seekers filled the courtroom. Several young ladies were among the crowd.

Formally charged with first-degree murder, Ferrell was asked how he wanted to plead. He replied in a strong, firm tone, "I am not guilty and will waive examination." Hamilton ordered him held in the Union County jail without bond. There were already ten prisoners on the first floor of the jail, so detectives led Ferrell to a cell on the second story, the women's floor. As he walked to his cell, the ten prisoners sang: "I'll leave my happy home for you."

When the contingency from Columbus left to go home, Ferrell turned morose and began crying for his mother and talking about suicide. He collapsed, and the guards sent for a doctor. The county commissioners authorized an around-the-clock watch to keep him from doing himself in. He asked the sheriff if he could have a matron instead of male guards. He claimed to get along better with women than men. The sheriff denied the request.

Ferrell spent most of the next few days writing letters to his sweetheart. His brother, Charles, came to visit one day, bringing a letter from his mother.

Police and reporters were surprised at the interest he spurred among young ladies. One day, he received a booklet of prayers with a note that

Ferrell was tried at the Union County Courthouse in Marysville. *Marysville Public Library.*

read, "Ask God to save your soul." The note was signed by M. and K. He apparently knew who sent it. Several women called at the jail with roses, but they were not allowed to see him. White and pink carnations with cards from two Columbus girls also arrived. The sheriff showed him the flowers and then returned them to the senders.

On September 12, Ferrell was arraigned before Judge Charles M. Melhorn. His plea was "not guilty." James E. Robinson and ex–probate judge James McCampbell would prosecute the case. R.L. Woodburn and Richard Cameron were appointed as defense counsel. Robinson, McCampbell and Cameron were all young men. Woodburn was older, but this was the first murder trial for all four. The Woodburn-and-Cameron team decided to enter a plea of not guilty by reason of insanity.

The trial opened at 9:00 a.m. on Monday, October 15, and the *Union County Journal* and *Marysville Tribune* covered each day. The case had drawn so much interest that it took two and a half days to seat an impartial jury. Once the proceedings got underway, the courtroom was packed to capacity, and hundreds stood in the hallways and corridors of the courthouse. People came from all over the state just to get a look at Rosslyn Ferrell as he was led into court handcuffed.

The prosecutors took the jury through the crime using sixty-one witnesses to tell the story. Most of those witnesses were detectives, express agents and railroad men. Ferrell's lawyers vigorously cross-examined each of these witnesses but did not gain much ground for their client.

At times, Ferrell seemed indifferent to the situation, showing no remorse or interest in the proceedings.

Louisa Lane, the murdered man's widow, was the prosecution's most dramatic witness. She was accompanied into the courtroom by her father-in-law and her tiny child. Ferrell gave her a cursory glance as she passed him on her way to the stand. Dressed in all black, she was a small, pathetic figure as she testified about her ten-year marriage to Lane. "I last saw him August 8," she said with bowed head. "My husband was in the express business for about ten years. He was from Illinois originally." She fidgeted with a handkerchief in her hands. "We have a sixteen-month-old son, Charles J. We moved to 246 West Fourth Avenue in Columbus just over a month before he died."

Prosecutors asked Louisa to identify her husband's bloody clothing as the same he was wearing when he left home. She looked at it, grew pale and nearly fainted. The defense counsel declined to cross-examine her, and she left the stand in tears.

The trial was interrupted for three days while one of the jurors recovered from a case of the measles. Hilina Ferrell, the accused's mother, took this opportunity to pay a visit to Louisa Lane. She begged the widow to retake the stand and tell the jury that she forgave Rosslyn Ferrell. Louisa treated the request with contempt and said she would never forgive him for killing her husband.

Woodburn and Cameron used their twenty-eight defense witnesses to paint Ferrell as a very troubled, depressed young man. They were going to try to save him from the electric chair with the contention that he was born with a hereditary "taint."

The first defense witness was Ferrell's great-aunt. She told the jury that his mother and father were first cousins, their mothers being sisters. Woodburn and Cameron put more relatives on the stand to corroborate this testimony and reveal more family skeletons. Their aim was to show that insanity ran in the bloodlines. One relative divulged that the family had several suicides and that there were other members who were confined to insane asylums.

Defense counsel brought in witnesses from Steubenville who had known Ferrell from the time he was a boy. They all said the same thing: he was of good character but not sound mind. He had a mental condition, and he always seemed timid and somewhat peculiar.

Miss Lillian Costlow was engaged to Rosslyn Ferrell. *Illustration by Justin Campbell.*

Even a former sweetheart testified that when she saw him three weeks prior to the killing, she noticed he "acted rather queerly."

Several of the witnesses stated that Ferrell was despondent in the few weeks leading up to the wedding date.

Ferrell's mother testified that she took him out of school at age nine on the advice of a physician because he was developing physically faster than mentally. "He often complained of head pains, and he was despondent the last time he visited," she said. Under cross-examination, she broke down and wept.

Lillian Costlow came to the stand wearing a grey skirt and jacket with a pink waist. A large black hat partially obscured her beautiful face. All eyes in the courtroom were riveted on her as she calmly told of her engagement to Ferrell. They had met in May 1899 and been engaged just about a year. "I am a Catholic. At my behest, Rosslyn was taking instructions to become a Catholic so we could be married in the Church," she told the court. She often accompanied him to his lesson. "A couple weeks before our wedding, I noticed his appearance change. He was melancholy, and he complained of having pains in his head. I did not know he was out of work and broke." Looking back, she remembered the look in his eyes was unnatural. When asked if she thought he was mentally deranged, she said, "Now, I do." She showed no distress under cross-examination. Answering the questions calmly, she related how the two of them went shopping after the murder.

When Julia Costlow, Lillian's mother, came to testify, she stated that Ferrell had called to see her daughter every evening for the month before his arrest. "I noticed that he was despondent," she said. "He had a wild and unnatural look in his eyes, and he complained of head pains." Under cross-examination, she said she was aware that her son-in-law-to-be was out of a job. "I felt alarmed, but we still would have permitted the wedding to take place." Ferrell and her daughter were to live independently in the Costlow home.

On redirect, Julia said, "I went to see him in jail because I cared for him, and I don't believe he was responsible for his act."

The defense called two different doctors to the stand. Both had talked with Ferrell when he collapsed at different times. Neither doctor could say decisively that he was insane. They both stated that intermarriage of relatives did not necessarily have a bad effect if there had been no more such relations in the family. Ferrell's lawyers also entered passages from books by authorities on insanity that seemed to fit their client's actions.

In his closing argument, Prosecutor James McCampbell picked up the murder gun and held it for the jury to see again. He talked of how Ferrell sat in his room at Montfort's boardinghouse with the gun, cleaning it and testing it to make sure it would fire when he needed it to. "He clicked it several times. His landlady heard it." Then McCampbell set the gun down, reached for the bloodstained clothing and held it up for the jury. "The last time Mrs. Lane saw her husband alive, he was wearing these." Ferrell lowered his head, and his mother covered her eyes with her handkerchief.

It was the defense's turn to present its closing argument next, and E.L. Woodburn rose to speak. He started by giving a history of how crimes had been punished in the country with barbaric treatment and had by degrees been modified and modernized. He cited a recently passed law of how juries could recommend mercy in first-degree murder verdicts.

In addition to recalling the Ferrell family's dark secrets for the jurors' ears, he detailed the accused's life from boyhood to his employment at Adams Express. To bolster his argument, he read from a medical work that claimed a mental disease could lie dormant for years in an insane person before manifesting itself.

Woodburn claimed that Rosslyn Ferrell was not responsible for his actions on the night of August 10, 1900, and he went back through the accused's life of deviant behavior. "But gentlemen," he addressed the jury, "if you do feel that he was [responsible] upon the evidence produced, you can still allow him a recommendation of mercy."

The jury took about seven hours and several ballots to decide Charles R.H. Ferrell's fate. When they filed back into court with their verdict, the room was so crowded that at least one woman passed out from the "impure air." The verdict was guilty of first-degree murder. The judge polled the jurors, and two recommended mercy. The trial had consumed sixteen days at a cost of $7,500. It was the biggest case in Union County's history.

Rosslyn Ferrell was sentenced to die in the electric chair.

Neither an appeal by Ferrell's attorneys nor a pleading letter to Governor George K. Nash from his mother would save his life.

On the day before Ferrell died, he visited with his brothers and asked that his watch be given to his mother. His final meals were porterhouse steak and mushrooms, chicken with oyster dressing and strawberries and cream and sliced tomatoes. He wrote a last letter to Lillian. She did not visit, but she sent a final message to him with her brother. However, her brother was not on the visitors' list, so Ferrell never got her message. He said prayers with two priests who had become his almost constant companions. One of the prison doctors visited him and asked if there was anything he could do for him. Ferrell answered, "There is only one thing I want to ask, doctor. I want you to make sure I am good and dead."

Ferrell was strapped in the electric chair and executed on Friday, March 1, 1901, at 12:05 a.m. He was the ninth man to die in Ohio's electric chair. His last request was to be buried in a black suit in a purple-lined coffin.

Rosslyn Ferrell died in the electric chair on March 1, 1901, at 12:05 a.m. *Columbus Metropolitan Library.*

Ferrell's body was shipped via Panhandle No. 6 to his home in Steubenville, where a crowd of nearly 1,500 morbidly curious people waited to catch a glimpse of his coffin as it was transferred from the baggage car to a waiting ambulance. Lillian Costlow and her mother, Julia, heavily veiled, descended the steps of the train and hurried to a cab.

Panhandle No. 6 carried Ferrell's coffin home to Steubenville. *Columbus Metropolitan Library.*

Hundreds of people followed the ambulance to the Ferrell home and later swarmed the house. Two policemen tried to control the crowd. Large orders of flowers were delivered and filled the house. The Costlows' arrangement was composed of lilies and red carnations.

CHAPTER 9

LOOT SOLD CHEAP

Looting freight cars became such a lucrative business in 1918 in Sharonville at the Cleveland, Cincinnati, Chicago & St. Louis (Big Four) railroad yard that area public officials may have had a hand in the plot. Whispers of politicians' involvement either as thieves themselves or as recipients of "gifts" from the boxcar booty lingered on people's lips. The thievery probably went on unchecked for over a year before city and private railroad detectives took action and U.S. Marshals joined the investigation.

Entire freight-car shipments were carried off in automobiles and wagons and stowed away in stables, barns, homes and stores. Merchandise had even been buried in the rail yards. Goods of every description, including automobile tires, butter, cigarettes, liquor, turkey and shoes, with an estimated value of $100,000 were pilfered from the cars. Several merchants were involved, having bought the stolen swag at low prices and sold it at big profits.

St. Bernard detectives Louis Bell and Joseph Schaefer were on the trail of the thieves and began arresting several men in April. Private Detectives Cal Crim and Paul Ryan of the Cal Crim Detective Bureau, as well as Big Four detectives Captain Breen and Taylor, also helped track down the offenders and recover the wares. Authorities did such a good job recovering the merchandise that they packed one whole room from top to bottom with the stolen goods.

Cincinnati merchant Abraham Wiener was arrested when lawmen traced twenty-six pairs of shoes and other clothing from the Sharonville rail yard to the upstairs of his home. That same day, Benjamin Adler, who owned a men's furnishing store at 1211 Central Avenue, was found with twenty-four suits that were part of the boxcar spoils. He told officers he bought the suits from Joseph Ginsberg for five dollars each. Ginsberg, a thirty-three-year-old tailor, claimed he was just an agent for Wiener and was paid a twenty-dollar commission for each suit he sold. Forty-two-year-old Wiener decided not to go to trial and pleaded guilty to receiving stolen goods. He was sentenced to sixty days. He also paid fifty dollars in fines plus court costs.

Private Detectives Crim and Ryan recovered twelve cases of whiskey and gin and enough cigarettes for a collective worth of $500 from a barbershop owned by George Kolman at 101 Mills Street. Suspicious that there was even more booty at the shop, the two detectives started knocking on the walls and floor until they heard a hollow sound. Underneath the linoleum floor covering was trapdoor. When pulled open, it revealed a compartment filled with automobile goods.

Police asserted that several other men were peddling dressed turkeys by the dozen at "ridiculously low prices" over the winter to people in the surrounding countryside. The looters were also selling sixty-pound tubs of butter for ten cents a pound.

Near the middle of April, detectives surrounded the Twelve-Mile House, also known as the Sharon House and Hotel Sharon, and found six men uncovering some of the booty from a tanbark (used to tan hides) pile. They were loading it into an automobile, probably to sell elsewhere. The detectives recovered clothing, cloth, dried fruits, groceries, automobile tires and twenty-three cartons of cigarettes stolen from the shipments of W. Duke & Sons. Searching further, they found stolen liquor in the hotel basement. The hotel served liquor. Added up, the merchandise was worth $2,000.

One in the group was a trainman who told the detectives how the merchandise had been stolen from the railroad cars. He said they packed the items into cars and onto wagons in order to take them to different hiding places around Sharonville, mostly stables and barns. Other railroad employees, he said, were in on the operation.

The men all complied with police except twenty-two-year-old James Green, who tried to make a run for it. Private Detective Jack Griffith chased after him for a mile. Several shots were reportedly fired, but Green was taken into custody without harm.

Green and twenty-eight-year-old George H. Weis were both from St. Bernard. Also arrested were Sharonville residents Wade H. Webb, William J. Wright, Edward J. Sellers and Elmer W. Vossler.

The Twelve-Mile House (Hotel Sharon) is on the National Register of Historic Places. It was a hiding place for stolen goods in 1918. *Society of Historic Sharonville.*

Vossler, thirty-four, was the proprietor of the Hotel Sharon. A week after the proprietor's arrest, Charles L. Swain, the attorney for the Anti-Saloon League, filed a protest against Vossler with the Hamilton County Liquor License Board for failing to conduct his establishment in a legal manner. Other saloon owners were mentioned in that protest, too, but Vossler's arrest most likely played a large part in that issue.

Webb was a thirty-seven-year-old brakeman with the railroad and could have been the one who offered information to the arresting officers.

Green, Kolman, Wiener, Sellers, Webb, Weis and Vossler had all been charged under an Ohio state statute of grand larceny for receiving stolen goods and were taken before Municipal Judge Fox on April 26. All of their charges were dismissed, but their troubles were not over. Waiting to snap the handcuffs on them for federal charges in violation of interfering with interstate shipments were the Deputy U.S. Marshals. The prisoners were marched off to the Federal Building.

George Kolman of Lockland was indicted on the federal charge on December 20, 1918. The U.S. district attorney claimed Kolman knew the twelve cases of whiskey—each holding twelve quarts—in his possession were stolen from the interstate rails. In January 1919, his bail was set for $1,000, but he was allowed to go free on his own recognizance. In June 1920, the U.S. district attorney entered a *nolle prosequi*, and the case was dismissed. The reason was not set out.

That same day, thirty-four-year-old Sellers, a railroad switchman, faced a charge in federal court of stealing a keg of whiskey and a keg of brandy. In March, he made a motion to the court to dismiss the charges. He argued that he had already faced the charges in state court, and they had been dropped. The motion was denied, and the U.S. district attorney's office set about getting ready for trial. Preparation included having Vossler testify against Sellers. In December 1919, Sellers finally pleaded guilty and was sentenced to thirty days in the Dayton Jail in Montgomery County.

The U.S. district attorney was not finished with Sellers. The government still wanted him to face charges along with thirty-four-year-old Walter Wright. The duo would face the judge for having possession of eleven cases of cigarettes—all filched from a Big Four freight car.

At first, Wright tried to get his case dismissed on the same grounds that Sellers did. He got the same results, so both he and Sellers pleaded guilty. Sellers was put in jail until he could come up with half the court costs. Wright got away with no jail time as long as he paid the other half of the court costs plus twenty dollars.

Webb, Vossler, Green and Weis were all indicted on the same day. The charge was being in possession of stolen goods from interstate rails, namely two cases of whiskey and six cases of cigarettes. Bond was set at different amounts ranging up to $1,500. All four walked out of the courthouse that day. Weis tried to get the charges dismissed because he had already faced them at the state level. He had as much luck as Sellers and Wright. In June 1920, the federal charges were dropped against Vossler, and a year later, they were dropped against Weis. Webb and Green both pleaded guilty and were given sixty and thirty days, respectively, in the jail at Dayton.

Trainmaster Harry Dunbar had been in trouble the year before when the thirty-four-year-old and six other trainmen were indicted for attacking another trainman from West Virginia. No disposition of that case was found, and apparently he never had to answer for his part in the boxcar thefts. Neither did Arthur Neff, a clerk from Sharonville.

Charles O. Brown, a railroad brakeman from Alabama, was arrested in January 1919 and turned over to federal authorities. He was caught taking twenty-one quarts of whiskey stashed in valises over state lines to Mobile, Alabama. He apparently never went to trial either.

William Knox was no stranger to law enforcement. He and a pal had been arrested for fighting with four men on the Cincinnati streets one Saturday night in December 1917. It took four police officers to subdue the pair.

When it came to the federal charges for the freight thefts, thirty-five-year-old Knox pleaded guilty. He was sentenced to one day in jail.

In all, police rounded up eighteen merchants and railroad employees who were connected to the ring in one way or another, but only eight faced the judge. The *Cincinnati Post* explained that there were others "implicated in the workings of the ring" but that they were not arrested because they provided information to the detectives in order to save themselves. An article in the *Cincinnati Enquirer* suggested political favors might have played a role in light sentences or no charges at all.

CHAPTER 10
PUBLIC ENEMY NUMBER ONE EXECUTES LAST GREAT TRAIN ROBBERY

By mid-1935, all the most notorious gangsters and killers were either in the big house or six feet under—all but Alvin "Creepy" Karpis, who picked up his nickname because of his sinister smile and cold stare.

Born Francis Albin Karpowicz in 1907 in Canada, he started out as a two-bit hood but made a name for himself in the early 1930s when he and Fred Barker robbed banks throughout the Midwest. Even more brazen, the Karpis-Barker Gang pulled off two kidnappings. One was the president of a bank, and the other was the president of a brewing company.

Karpis found himself promoted to the number-one spot on J. Edgar Hoover's Public Enemy list after Doc Barker was captured in Chicago on January 8, 1935, and Fred and Ma Barker were gunned down in a four-hour shootout in Florida a week or so later.

That summer was a hot one for Karpis—not just because of the weather, but because the FBI was breathing down his neck. He was on the lam, but robbery ran in his veins. He considered it his job, and he longed for a big, spectacular heist. According to his autobiography, *The Alvin Karpis Story*, written with Bill Trent, he got the idea of holding up a train from stories he had read about the Wild West and the James-Younger Gang.

After much consideration, he locked focus on a mail train that carried payrolls from Cleveland, Ohio, to the Republic Steel Mill in Warren. As a bonus, it also carried payrolls for the mills in both Youngstown and Pittsburgh. He figured the job would net at least as much as the bank robberies he and Fred Barker had pulled—maybe more.

Alvin Karpis (right) and Larry O'Keefe were captured in 1930 in Kansas City with these guns. *Acme Newspictures Inc., Cleveland Press Collection, CSU Michael Schwartz Library.*

It took Karpis weeks to case the train. Finally, he decided the best place to hit it would be the Erie Railroad depot at Garrettsville. He was meticulous when planning any robbery, but this one was special. Every last detail had to be perfect. He went over the scheme again and again, looking for any flaws. The best part would be the escape, and it would involve an airplane.

The Garrettsville Station where Karpis and his gang robbed a mail train no longer stands. *Cleveland Press Collection, CSU Michael Schwartz Library.*

Next, Karpis chose his accomplices. Freddie Hunter and Harry Campbell were old pals and, most importantly, experienced. Fifty-year-old Ben Grayson was just out of prison for a post-office robbery, and Sam Coker also had some jobs under his belt. John Brock was new, but he came highly recommended by Karpis's friend "Burrhead" Keady.

On Thursday, November 7, 1935, when Erie Railroad train No. 626 ground to a halt at 2:15 p.m., two minutes late, Karpis and his bandits, armed with machine guns, automatic pistols and a sawed-off shotgun, stepped out of a brand-new Plymouth and onto the station platform in Garrettsville and took their positions.

Newspaper accounts told of six robbers, but Karpis claimed there were only five. Coker, who was originally assigned to watch the moneybags being loaded at the Federal Reserve in Cleveland, had come down with the clap and was out of commission.

Witnesses said two of the men wore masks. One wore a black silk handkerchief over the upper part of his face. The other had a white handkerchief over the lower part of his face and glasses covering his eyes. This one could have been Karpis, as he sometimes wore glasses.

Karpis held up an Erie train in 1935 at the Garrettsville Station. *Cleveland Press Collection, CSU Michael Schwartz Library.*

According to Karpis, Ben Grayson showed up for the job in a comical disguise of a droopy moustache and rouge on his cheeks. Having just been released from prison, Grayson wanted to be certain no one recognized him. Disguise or not, Grayson got the drop on Engineer Charles Shull and Fireman P.O. Leuschner and ordered them down from the cab, keeping them close to the engine and under cover of a gun.

The station agent, W.B. Moses, and an Erie telephone lineman, Carl Clutter, were both inside the freight office when the robbery occurred, according to a *Cleveland Plain Dealer* report. Suddenly, one of the robbers—most likely John Brock—appeared in the office window, brandishing a machine gun. "Get outside. Get outside quick or I'll shoot," he snarled at them. Clutter complied, but Moses slammed the door, locked it and then hid in a corner.

Mrs. W.L. Scott, a Garrettsville resident, was at the station to post a letter to her husband. She got the surprise of her life when she heard a voice behind her say, "Stick 'em up." She turned and saw the barrel of an automatic pistol pointed right at her. Earl N. Davis, a Garrettsville news agent, thought it was some kind of joke when he heard the same words from over his shoulder. He turned to find that it was no joke.

Station cashier Fred Ball was up on the mail truck unloading mail and packages when one of the robbers waved a machine gun at him and ordered him to get down and line up with the others. Scott, Davis, Ball and anyone else around were quickly lined up on the platform and made to hold their hands high in the air.

Karpis saved the starring role in this production for himself. He stepped out of the shiny new getaway car wearing a topcoat with the pocket ripped out. Slung over his shoulder underneath the coat was a machine gun fitted with his preferred twenty-shot clip. He also brought along a few dynamite sticks—just in case. He confidently strode to the mail car, swung his gun from under his coat and leveled it at the clerks in the car. He ordered them to throw their hands up. Much to his surprise, they did not raise their hands but instead dashed back into the darkness of the car.

Karpis had not counted on this degree of resistance, especially since he was holding a machine gun. He pulled out a stick of dynamite. Just as he was about to toss it into the car, he glanced over and saw that Freddie Hunter, who was supposed to be keeping an eye on the parking lot, had taken off after a couple of tramps who were running down the track. The next thing Karpis knew, a car engine started. He whirled toward the parking lot, which was only a few yards away, and saw a man and woman trying to escape in a car. If they got away, the whole thing could fall apart. He made his decision quickly and ran to the car. Flinging open the driver's door, he yelled, "Get the hell out of the car!" He reached in, ripped the keys

J. Edgar Hoover considered Karpis so dangerous that he named him Public Enemy Number One. *Cleveland Press Collection, CSU Michael Schwartz Library.*

Karpis's official police mug shot after his capture in New Orleans. *Cleveland Press Collection, CSU Michael Schwartz Library.*

from the ignition and hurled them across the parking lot.

Karpis dashed back to the platform, but the mail clerks still had not shown their faces. He lobbed an unlit dynamite stick into the darkness of the car. That failed to flush them out. He then threatened to light a second stick and started to count to five. The threat worked, and three mail clerks emerged from the back of the car. Karpis had thought there were only two clerks. Two of the clerks were white. The third clerk Karpis described as a defiant, heavy-set black man. "He was a nervy son-of-a-bitch," Karpis wrote. And not one of the three would put his hands in the air.

According to Karpis, he tried to fire a shot over the clerks' heads, but the gun did not go off. He claimed the sound of the hammer scared them enough, and they finally raised their hands. This was contrary to what Ball told the newspapers. One report claimed that one of the clerks was slightly grazed in the forehead. "I heard a shot fired in the mail car," the station cashier said. "It was only a shot to frighten the clerks and was not aimed at anyone so far as I could see." Karpis then asked which one of the men was the chief clerk. The older man stepped forward, and Karpis ordered him back into the mail car. The scene inside the car was daunting to Karpis. He was faced with floor-to-ceiling mail sacks, and the clerk showed no inclination to help sort through them. Karpis again trained his gun on the clerk and reminded him that another train was due to come down the track very soon and that it would ram into this train. In his biography, it was written that he said, "There'll be a lot of people dead. I don't care about that, but you might."

At that, the clerk relented and hunted out the Warren payroll, which was in a bag with a heavy padlock. "Where's the other sack, the one from the Federal Reserve Bank?" Karpis asked.

"It isn't here."

Karpis did not believe him and again threatened him with the gun. Just then, Harry jumped on the car. Karpis turned to him and told him to look out because he was going to shoot the old man if he did not hand over the Youngstown payroll. The clerk then went to his desk and produced his ledger, proving that he had signed for only one payroll shipment. Apparently, the Youngstown payroll had shipped out the day before.

In a fit of anger, Karpis grabbed five more bags of registered mail in hopes that something of value would be in them. He and Freddie then ordered the clerks to load them in the back of the getaway car.

Mrs. Scott told the newspapers that the robbers made the clerks carry the mailbags over to the car. "I saw one of the robbers pick up one of the mail bags," she said. "He used only his thumb and index finger and was mighty careful. It looked as if he was being very careful that he didn't get any fingerprints on it."

The robbers were careful not to leave fingerprints, except for Karpis, who had no fingerprints; they had been removed by underworld plastic surgeon Joseph Moran in March 1933. The operation was so successful that many years later, Karpis had trouble obtaining a passport to return to his native Canada.

When ordered to carry the mailbags, one big clerk balked. With some incentive by way of a foot in the back from Hunter, the clerk grabbed the bags. Davis was ordered out of the line to help load the getaway car. As he dumped four of the sacks at their car, he got a glimpse inside and saw two more machine guns and two or three automatic pistols on the floor.

According to Karpis, the whole robbery took only a few minutes, and the passengers were none the wiser.

Apparently, none of the robbers saw a woman get off the train. According to the *Garrettsville*

Young Karpis was considered a public enemy. An older Karpis was paroled after thirty-three years. *Cleveland Press Collection, CSU Michael Schwartz Library.*

Journal, a woman ran to the back of the train and headed across the tracks to A.D. Sheperd's coal-yard office. The man in the office notified the telephone operator of the holdup. The operator already knew about the robbery and had notified the Garrettsville marshal. The first alarm had come from a woman visiting a friend who lived near the station.

When the Federal Reserve Bank tallied its losses, C.W. Arnold, the assistant deputy governor of the Cleveland bank, told reporters that the train carried $39,500 in currency that was consigned to a Warren bank and $12,450 in securities. He said the robbers took $34,000 but overlooked $5,500 in cash. The money was to be used for payroll for the Republic Steel works. Postmaster Michael F. O'Donnell said that six or seven mail pouches were stolen but that only three contained registered mail. One of the bags contained cash on its way to Warren, and the other two contained the securities bound for Pittsburgh. Although the cash money was taken, Republic Steel said it would meet its obligation to the workers by check.

Karpis knew he couldn't hide out in Ohio after the robbery. The feds already had an idea he was somewhere in the state even before he knocked over the train. For that reason, the escape was one of the most meticulous he had ever planned. He took great care in his choice of a getaway car. He wanted a four-door Ford with a V-8 engine, but there were none to be had in the area. He even offered one car dealer an extra $100 if he could locate one. In the end, he had to settle for the Plymouth.

Karpis planned a getaway route that was full of turn-backs and twists. He had practiced it so many times before the robbery that he knew every bump in the road. The route carried them from Garrettsville north to Port Clinton, where there was a small airport. He was pleased with how well the robbery went and with their escape. The disappointment set in when they tore open the payroll bag and mail sacks. The haul totaled no more than $34,000, according to Karpis. He had expected far more. According to his autobiography, in the end, he congratulated himself for pulling off a train robbery "in fine style just like the famous old Western bandits."

Karpis had purchased a light Stinson plane and hired a pilot named John Zetzer. The morning after the robbery, Zetzer had the plane warmed up and ready to fly Karpis and Hunter to Hot Springs, Arkansas, and into the arms of their girlfriends there. Karpis gave the plane to Zetzer after the trip and handed him $500 to get rid of the Plymouth.

Karpis had a fondness for prostitutes, particularly madams. He kept company for some time with Grace Goldstein, who ran a bordello called the Hatterie Hotel in Hot Springs. After the train robbery, the two took off on

Above: Hoover is in the foreground as Karpis is being led into court in St. Paul. *Acme Newspictures Inc., Cleveland Press Collection, CSU Michael Schwartz Library.*

Right: After prison, Karpis, shown here with attorney James Carty, was deported to Canada. *Acme Newspictures Inc., Cleveland Press Collection, CSU Michael Schwartz Library.*

vacation to Florida. She claimed to have married him in September 1935 in New York, but no documents were ever found to back up that claim.

On May 1, 1936, as Karpis was walking to his car in New Orleans, he was arrested by the FBI. J. Edgar Hoover claimed to have made the arrest himself, but Karpis told a different story.

After thirty-three years in prison for kidnapping and train robbery, Karpis was paroled and deported back to Canada. Three years later, he moved to Spain, where he died in 1979. He was seventy-two years old.

SOURCES

BOOKS

Columbus Police Benevolent Association. *History of the Police Department of Columbus, Ohio*. Columbus, OH: Columbus Police Benevolent Association, 1908.

Fornshell, Marvin E. *The Historical and Illustrated Ohio Penitentiary*. Columbus, OH: 1908.

Foster, Thomas E., and Alonzo B. Shaw. *Trails in Shadow Land: Stories of a Detective*. Columbus, OH: Hann and Adair Printing Co., 1910.

Karpis, Alvin, and Bill Trent. *The Alvin Karpis Story*. New York: Coward, McCann & Geoghegan, 1971.

McKinnon, Isaiah. *In the Line of Duty: A Tribute to Fallen Law Enforcement Officers from the State of Michigan*. Paducah, KY: Turner Publishing Company, 2003.

Merriman, Scott. *The Great Sharonville Train Robbery, Parts 1 & 2*. Sharonville, OH: Society of Historic Sharonville, 1997.

Portrait and Biographical Record of Auglaize, Logan and Shelby Counties, Ohio; Containing Biographical Sketches of Prominent and Representative Citizens, Together with Biographies and Portraits of All the Presidents of the United States. Chicago: Chapman Brothers, 1892.

Sources

Roe, George M. *Our Police: A History of the Cincinnati Police Force, from the Earliest Period Until the Present Day.* New York: AMS Press Inc., 1976.

Yenne, Bill. *Atlas of North American Railroads.* St. Paul, MN: MBI Publishing Co., 2005.

PERIODICALS

Akron Beacon Journal
Ann Arbor Argus
Bellefontaine Examiner
Bellefontaine Republican
Bend of the River (Maumee, OH)
Buffalo Courier
Canton Repository
Champaign Democrat
Chicago Inter Ocean
Chicago Post and Mail
Cincinnati Commercial Tribune
Cincinnati Enquirer
Cincinnati Gazette
Cincinnati Post
Cleveland Leader
Cleveland Plain Dealer/Plain Dealer
Cleveland Press
Columbus Citizen
Columbus Dispatch
Courier Journal (Louisville, KY)
Crestline Advocate
Daily Herald (Delphos, OH)
Danville Daily Democrat
Danville Daily News
Elkhart Evening Review
Evening Argus (Owosso, MI)
Hoopeston Daily Chronicle (Hoopeston, IL)
Indianapolis Sentinel
Journal-News (Hamilton, OH)
Marysville Tribune

Sources

Massillon Item
New York Herald
New York Times
Pittsburgh Dispatch
Plain City Advocate
Springfield Daily Republic
Summit County Beacon
Union County Journal (Marysville, OH)
West Liberty Banner

WEBSITES AND OTHER SOURCES

FBI.gov. "Alvin Francis Karpis." http://vault.fbi.gov/alvin-francis-karpis.

State of Ohio Penitentiary Records, Register of Prisoners.

Turzillo, Jane A. "Hot Springs Madam Harbored Public Enemy No. 1." http://darkheartedwomen.wordpress.com.

United States Federal Census, 1870, 1880, 1900.

Unpublished Partial Transcript, *State of Ohio v. Charles H. "Blinky" Morgan*, Portage County Common Pleas Court, 1887.

INDEX

ABOUT THE AUTHOR

Courtesy of LBJ Photography.

Jane Ann Turzillo writes about Ohio history and true crime; *Murder and Mayhem on Ohio's Rails* combines the two. Her previous book, *Wicked Women of Northeast Ohio*, was also published by The History Press. As one of the original owners of a large weekly newspaper in Northeast Ohio, she covered police news and wrote a historical crime column. She has won several Ohio Professional Writers (Ohio Press Women) awards for fiction and nonfiction. She has taught writing on the college level and is the author of two more historical books. Ms. Turzillo holds degrees in criminal justice technology and mass-media communication from the University of Akron. She is a member of Mystery Writers of America, Sisters in Crime and the National Federation of Press Women. When not engrossed in researching and writing, she is possessed by photography.

Visit us at
www.historypress.net

....

This title is also available as an e-book